REF
PN
99
.G7   Needham, H. A. ed.
N4
1969   Taste and criticism
Cop.1   in the eighteenth
           century

12.25

DATE		
	REFERENCE	

TASTE AND CRITICISM IN THE EIGHTEENTH
CENTURY

A CLASSICAL LANDSCAPE: STOWE, BUCKINGHAMSHIRE

By permission of " Country Life "

Taste and Criticism in the Eighteenth Century

A Selection of Texts illustrating the Evolution of Taste and the Development of Critical Theory

EDITED BY

H. A. NEEDHAM D. de l'U.

Select Bibliographies Reprint Series

BOOKS FOR LIBRARIES PRESS
FREEPORT, NEW YORK

First published 1952 as part of the Life,
Literature, & Thought Library by
George G. Harrap & Co. Ltd.

Reprinted 1969 by arrangement

STANDARD BOOK NUMBER:
8369-5035-6

LIBRARY OF CONGRESS CATALOG CARD NUMBER:
71-80624

PRINTED IN THE UNITED STATES OF AMERICA

FOREWORD

THIS series aims at presenting in an attractive form English texts which have not only intrinsic merit as literature but which are also valuable as manifestations of the spirit of the age in which they were written. The plan was inspired by the desire to break away from the usual annotated edition of English classics and to provide a series of books illustrating some of the chief developments in English civilization since the Middle Ages. Each volume will have a substantial introduction, which will relate writers to the main currents of contemporary life and thought, and which will be an important part of the book. Notes, where given, will be brief, stimulating, and designed to encourage the spirit of research in the student. It is believed that these books will be of especial value to students in universities and the upper forms of schools, and that they will also appeal very much to the general reader.

Grateful acknowledgment is made of the valuable help given to the series in its early stages by Mr S. E. Buckley.

VIVIAN DE SOLA PINTO
General Editor,
Life, Literature
And Thought Library

PREFACE

THIS book is intended to serve as an introduction to the study of English literary criticism and æsthetic philosophy of the eighteenth century. It does not pretend to give an exhaustive account of either of these divisions of learning or to discuss fully the qualities of the individual authors represented; its object is rather to illustrate certain movements of doctrine, taste, and feeling, and to show some of the connexions between different aspects of the culture of the period.

An attempt is made in the Introduction to lay down the broad lines of this study, and to give some indications of the relationships existing between critical theory and the arts in this time. These hints are necessarily sketchy and incomplete, but it is hoped that the reader will be led to amplify them by extending the analysis to other forms of art, and by seeking illustrations of particular points in the resources available to him.

As the object of the book is to present a body of ideas (some of which are still effective in modern criticism and æsthetic) rather than to assemble a number of documents, complete freedom has been taken, where necessary, to arrange extracts from the same author among different sections of the text. For the same reason the spelling has been modernized throughout and the punctuation occasionally simplified.

No attempt has been made here to present a complete bibliography of this complex field, but a list is given of some books which will be found useful either for reference or for the further study of particular subjects. A full and classified bibliography of the literature and critical theory of the period will be found in the second volume of the *Cambridge Bibliography of English Literature*.

H. A. NEEDHAM

CONTENTS

INTRODUCTION

THE CHARACTER OF THE EIGHTEENTH CENTURY AND THE PLACE OF THE ARTS IN ITS CULTURE

TWENTIETH-CENTURY disillusionment may sometimes be heard comforting itself with the ironical remark that "after all, European civilization came to an end with the French Revolution!" Perhaps few of those who speak thus would have cared to live in eighteenth-century England, with its highwaymen and press-gangs, its lack of sanitation and frequent epidemics, its gin-shops, public executions, and transportations; yet, in spite of the grossness and brutality of some aspects of the life of that time, there is a sense in which this facetious statement about European civilization is true. There existed among the upper classes of Western Europe in the mid-eighteenth century a more stable and homogeneous culture than has been found at any time since the Industrial Revolution.

In the early nineteenth century a fashion grew up of ridiculing the preceding age: thus Carlyle spoke of it as "the age of prose, of lying, of sham; the fraudulent, bankrupt century; the reign of Beelzebub; the peculiar era of Cant." More recently, literary historians have often labelled the period the 'age of reason' in contrast to the Romantic period, which is seen as the age of poetry and imagination. But neither of these views is justified. The eighteenth century was not lacking in sentiment and in poetry, nor can it be denied that, with its widespread interest in art, letters, and philosophy, it achieved a high level of civilization. A modern historian gives it as his opinion that

> in spite of the decadence of the only two Universities that then existed in England, in spite of the decay of the endowed schools specially charged with secondary education, the intellectual life of the country was never more brilliant, and the proportion of men of genius per head of population in the irregularly educated England of George III was immensely greater than in our own day.[1]

Each of the three main divisions into which the eighteenth century naturally falls—the 'Augustan Age,' or period of Queen Anne and George I, the middle years, or 'Age of Johnson,' and the 'Revolutionary period,' from about 1775 to the turn of the century—was rich in great personalities. If we think only of the English art, drama, and literature of the central period, what a galaxy of names comes to mind! Johnson, Burke, Goldsmith, Sheridan, Boswell; Gray, Collins, Cowper; Richardson, Smollett, Fielding; Hume, Gibbon; Hogarth, Reynolds, Gainsborough, Richard Wilson; Horace Walpole; William Kent, Chippendale, Sir William Chambers, Robert Adam; Garrick and Mrs Siddons—these names indicate at once the richness and diversity of the culture of the age.

The civilization of the earlier part of the eighteenth century was aristocratic in basis. This was the last great age of patronage in art, and a time in which the noble patron was often himself an amateur in architecture or in some allied field of art. Foremost among such patrons was the Earl of Burlington (1695–1753), to whom Pope's "IVth Epistle" in the *Moral Essays* was addressed. The architects and designers of the Georgian era were not, indeed, in the same position of financial dependence as artists and men of letters had been in the Restoration period, and several of the great architects of the

[1] G. M. Trevelyan: *English Social History* (Longmans, 1944).

mid-century were able to amass considerable wealth. More-over, the Whig party was beginning to be alive to the desirability of the official use and encouragement of art. But it was still the tastes and needs of an aristocratic society that determined the scale and form of the chief works of the period.

Our recognition of the aristocratic nature of this art must not, however, be allowed to obscure our perception of the wider culture of the time. When we turn our attention from major architecture and the plastic arts to humbler forms of art or to literature it becomes clear that there existed at this time, through a broad stratum of society embracing both the gentry and the merchant class, a common body of artistic and literary knowledge and a general agreement in taste and culture.

The educated classes, especially in the middle portion of the century (from about 1740–75), were keenly interested in philosophic thought and in the artistic movements of their age. It must be admitted that they were sometimes deficient in spiritual insight and not greatly occupied with religious experience, and that they tended at first to overestimate the power of the intellect and to undervalue emotion; but they believed in their world, and attributed a high value to literature and art.

This eighteenth-century civilization had its centre in the towns, and particularly in the capital cities; but while London and Edinburgh were pre-eminent, they held no monopoly of culture, and provincial cities such as Bristol, Norwich, Coventry, Birmingham, York, and Newcastle were important centres of taste, learning, and talent. In this connexion it is noteworthy that, in contrast to the conditions that have pre-vailed in the last hundred years, the eighteenth-century town possessed all the advantages of a grouped population without being cut off from the surrounding countryside. The structure of society had not yet been shattered by the Industrial Revolu-tion, and this period presented a better balance between town and country, between intellectual activity and manual labour, than any age before or since.

The clearest illustrations of the taste of the age are probably to be found in its architecture, furniture, and interior decoration; and here we must consider not only extravagant examples of ducal splendour such as Vanbrugh's Blenheim Palace or Kent's Holkham House but also the city churches and the houses, streets, and squares of the period which remain (though often degraded) in London, Bristol, Bath, and many other English towns. The unpretentious style of the domestic building of the Queen Anne period, with its variety and simple ornament, though influenced to some extent by Dutch example, was the natural outcome of the native English tradition. The more severe Georgian manner, which developed as the century proceeded, was the last homogeneous 'school' of architecture produced in this country; for the nineteenth century, although a time of much experiment—in styles ranging from Regency classicism to revived Gothic—gave birth to little art which sprang naturally from the life and genius of contemporary society.

This diffusion of taste in eighteenth-century society was accompanied by a critical spirit and an interest in the philosophy of art and literature. It is not, therefore, surprising to find that the study of the branch of philosophy unhappily called 'æsthetics' was first organized in this period.

THE CRITICAL OUTLOOK OF THE FIRST HALF OF THE CENTURY

Complexity of Critical Movements. The literature of the early eighteenth century was much more complex in character and substance than appears at first sight.

It is at once obvious that much of this literature, like the architecture and decorative art of the time, was controlled by obedience to classical orthodoxy and 'squared by the rule of Greece and Rome'; and in the field of literary criticism it is possible to trace, in the succession of dominant literary figures of the first half of the century, a continuous presentation of neo-classic doctrine. The reign of Queen Anne saw the publication of Addison's critical essays in *The Spectator*, and of Pope's *Essay on Criticism*—the English counterpart of Boileau's famous *Art poétique* (1674), and the most brilliant formularization in this country of the orthodox view of poetry. Addison's critical essays in *The Spectator* (1711–12) helped to propagate the neo-classic creed (with some modifications) among a rapidly increasing reading public. Dr Johnson's criticism, in the middle years of the century, still embodied some elements of neo-classic doctrine, and in his *Discourses* Sir Joshua Reynolds expounded a revived classicism with reference to the art of painting.

This classical tradition is, however, only one element in the literature and criticism of the century; and, while it is right to look on the eighteenth century as predominantly classical in outlook, and misleading to think of a 'Romantic revolt' as taking place in the mind of Addison, or Hurd, or even of Thomas Warton, it is equally important to remember that none of the great 'classical' critics of the age expresses a purely classical doctrine. In all of them there are reservations and contradictions—of which they were often unaware—and it cannot be denied that the elements of what we call 'Romanticism' were present in our literary criticism from the time of Dryden. Pope and Addison were both in some respects 'Romantics,' and a number of writers of the next generation (in particular the Wartons, Young, and Bishop Hurd) developed these 'Romantic' lines of thought much more fully, but without regarding themselves as rebels against the inherited tastes of their age.

The Neo-classic Background. The main tenets of neo-classicism— principles that can be illustrated much more clearly in France than in England—might be expressed in the following terms. Reason, rather than imagination or sentiment, should be the dominant faculty in artistic creation. The primary interest of the poet or writer should be the psychological study of Man, and especially of Man in Society, and the subjects of literature should be drawn primarily from the Court and the city. The artist's treatment of his subject should be impersonal, rather than individualistic, and his work should be based on the close imitation of classical models. Art should be judged primarily on its technical perfection, rather than on its power to arouse emotion. The 'kinds,' or *genres*, in literature should be kept distinct—*i.e.*, tragedy and comedy, for example, should not be intermingled, and there should be a distinction between the language of poetry and that of prose. Finally, the function of literature (and especially of poetry) should be to please and to instruct.

The seventeenth century had set itself to apply these principles especially to drama and to epic or heroic poetry. In dramatic criticism particular stress was laid on the value of the 'Unities' and on the attainment of psychological truth and dramatic 'decorum.' In discussing the epic, critics had insisted chiefly on the need for the unity of the 'fable,' the proper diversity of episodes, the nobility of the hero, the clarity of the moral, and the propriety and richness of diction and ornament. Prose was naturally subject to critical prescription to a far less degree than poetry, but in prose also the main trend of the seventeenth century had been towards simplicity of form and clarity and elegance of expression.

Similar rules of composition were carried, moreover, into other fields of art, and especially into architecture, town planning, painting, the decorative arts, and garden design, and in these arts the classical impulse was perhaps stronger and more permanent in its effects than in the world of letters. Its force in the art of painting is shown by the long-lived prestige of Du Fresnoy's *De arte graphica* (1668). This book, with its neo-classic doctrine of painting—and, it may be noted, its insistence on the Horatian conception *Ut pictura poesis*— was first translated into English by Dryden in 1695. Further translations followed in the eighteenth century, the last being by the poet William Mason in 1783, with notes by Sir Joshua Reynolds.

Evidence of the persistence of the classical tradition in architecture is found in many great buildings, from Wren's work at Greenwich Hospital (begun in 1683) to Sir William Chambers's Somerset House (1788), and in the planning of Bath, and of the London squares. It is true that the following of neo-classic principles in architecture led sometimes to rigidity, and to the mere unimaginative reproduction of the details of Italian Renaissance buildings, but this classical style was in the main dignified and elegant, and characterized by a feeling of light and space. Qualities of elegance, form, and proportion became the designer's prime consideration.

The Place of Rationalism in Critical Theory. In literature and in literary criticism, however, other forces were at work from the earliest years of the century, forces which, while often apparently allied with neo-classic doctrine, were destined to assist in its overthrow. The first of these, which we may call 'Rationalism,' was fortified by the philosophy of Descartes in France and by the writings of Hobbes in England, and was an essential element in the classicism of the latter half of the seventeenth century.

Hobbes, in his famous *Answer* to Davenant's preface to *Gondibert* (1650), emphasized the importance, in the creative faculty of the poet, of Judgment, as opposed to Fancy. "Judgment," he says, "begets the strength and structure, and Fancy begets the ornaments of a Poem." The work of art, in his view, must be based on knowledge and truth; its content and its form are dependent on the exercise of judgment, and therefore the poet's first need is 'discretion' rather than

B

imagination. The artist should endeavour to present the truth of nature in its widest sense, and to penetrate to the laws governing both the external universe and the world of man and society. To do this he must be guided by Reason, or by 'Good Sense' or 'Common Sense.'

As the need for these qualities had been constantly stressed by the great classical critics (and particularly by Aristotle, Horace, and rhetoricians like Quintilian) it was easy for the seventeenth-century classicists to absorb this new rationalist doctrine and to reinforce their appeals to classical precedents by appeals to reason and good sense. Hence arose many of the famous clichés of neo-classic criticism, expressed so neatly by Boileau and by Pope:

> Quelque sujet qu'on traite, ou plaisant, ou sublime,
> Que toujours le bon sens s'accorde avec la rime.

> Aimez donc la raison. Que toujours, vos écrits
> Empruntent d'elle seule et leur lustre et leur prix.

> First follow Nature, and your judgment frame
> By her just standard, which is still the same.

> Those Rules of old discover'd, not deviz'd,
> Are Nature still, but Nature methodiz'd.

Dryden's earlier writings occasionally reflect this rationalist doctrine; but Dryden was rarely dogmatic in his outlook. The English critic who most whole-heartedly adopted the rationalist position was Thomas Rymer, who judged the merits of poetry primarily by its truth to nature, or its 'making sense.' He considered Reason to be the sole basis of the plot of a drama, and upon this doctrine built up his theory that tragedy should always illustrate poetic justice. The extremes to which a critic may go when guided only by pure reason or common sense are clearly seen in the chapter of Rymer's *Short View of Tragedy* (1693) in which he condemns *Othello*.

Rationalism was, however, a dangerous ally for neo-classic

theory. The assumption that the classical and the rational were necessarily equivalent was bound to be exploded sooner or later, and the literal rationalism of a critic such as Rymer could not long be regarded as the true criterion of artistic merit.

The Revival of Sentiment and the Conception of 'Taste.' The Influence of the Rediscovery of 'Longinus' on the Idea of Criticism and on Critical Practice. The constant stressing of the need for decorum and regularity in works of art tended to provoke a reaction in favour of feeling, enthusiasm, and more purely imaginative qualities. Writers and critics began to look for sentiment, grace, and charm, rather than reason and correctness. This literary trend had its counterpart in philosophy. Some of the most original thinkers of the early years of the century—Shaftesbury, Mandeville, Francis Hutcheson, and Bishop Butler—were primarily interested in the study of moral philosophy and of sentiment. In their view, philosophy had been too long concerned with the reason or understanding, and had neglected the study of the 'passions'—love, pride, anger, and the rest—by which the nature and spirit of man's thought was so much determined.

In the æsthetic sphere this new tendency, already clearly manifested in the literary criticism of the last decade of the seventeenth century, found its watchword in the new terms 'taste' or 'good taste'—terms first made current in England by Dryden, Saint-Évremond, and Temple, and then popularized by Addison and Shaftesbury. The word 'taste' was used somewhat loosely and with varying emphasis on sensibility or judgment, so that it is hardly just to speak, as has been done, of the 'School of Taste'; but there is no doubt about the importance of this new movement in æsthetic appreciation. It was the new elements constituting 'taste' that gave vitality and interest to literature and art in the early and middle eighteenth century.

The greatest single stimulus to this new trend came from

the dissemination of a knowledge of the ideas of the famous
essay *On the Sublime* (Περὶ Ὕψους (?)first century A.D.). This
essay, then ascribed to Longinus, was translated into French in
1674 by Boileau, who followed up this translation with *Critical
Reflections* on the work (1694). The fact that this treatise was
reintroduced to the modern world by a great modern 'classical'
critic shows how the elements of the newer conception of
taste combined with more traditional ways of thought. In
'Longinus' the seventeenth century found a master who,
while not underestimating the place in poetry and rhetoric
of the classical qualities of logic, decorum, and structure,
attached a still higher value to originality and the power
of moving reader and auditor. Though the full implications
of his doctrine were not realized at the time, much of his
spirit was perceived, and from the study of his work there
arose also a new conception of the function of the critic.
Henceforth the critic was to be regarded, not so much as a
judge, still less as a picker-out of faults, but rather as a revealer
of the 'beauties' of the work under examination. In English
criticism the influence of this work was first clearly seen in
Dryden's *Apology for Heroic Poetry* (1677), in which, besides
discussing the theory of the heroic poem, Dryden also dealt
with the qualifications of the critic and the methods proper to
criticism. The majority of Dryden's own essays exemplify
the new and liberal spirit of criticism, which many other
writers, from Steele, Addison, and Pope to Goldsmith, continued to advocate and to practise. It is noteworthy that, in
spite of the force of neo-classicism, and especially of French
seventeenth-century criticism, Dryden and the majority of
English eighteenth-century critics preserved a spirit of independence and breadth of judgment. These qualities were clear
tokens of their artistic sincerity.

*Small Importance of the Ancients and Moderns Controversy in
England: the Idea of Historical Criticism.* The growth of these

new critical ideas was accompanied in England by a more general realization of the meaning of history; and this explains why the Ancients and Moderns controversy, which at this time divided the literary world of France into two sharply opposed camps, had no serious counterpart in this country.

It is true that, apart from *Paradise Lost* and *Samson Agonistes*, England had produced no examples of modern classicism like the masterpieces of Corneille, Racine, and Molière, which invited comparison with the classics of the ancient world, and that the main problem of the French controversy did not therefore arise; but the difference between the literary evolution of the two countries was more radical than this. English critics, such as Dryden, realized that the true critical problem of the late Renaissance lay not in the comparison of modern classical works with their antique models, but in the whole relationship between modern art and the supposed authority of the classics.

For this reason, although most Elizabethan critics had stressed the value of classical precedents, and although many of the academic and fashionable writers of the eighteenth century continued to insist on an even more rigid form of classical doctrine, English thought in the seventeenth and eighteenth centuries never succumbed to classical domination. As early as 1602 Daniel had claimed the right of the nations of modern Europe to develop their own poetic genius independently of the methods of classical antiquity, and Bacon, in his *Advancement of Learning* (1605), had shown the significance of the historical growth of man's intellect and artistic genius. As early as 1668 Dryden, in his *Essay of Dramatic Poetry*, showed the futility of trying to measure Shakespeare's value by classical rules, and in his preface to the *Third Miscellany* and *Heads of an Answer to Rymer* he claimed, even more boldly, that modern English dramatists, and Shakespeare in particular, had achieved perfection in a richer form of drama than that known to the Greeks, and had done so in part because they had "written to the genius of the age and nation in which they lived." Therefore, he argued, the true critic should judge their work in relation to the spirit and conditions of seventeenth-century England; "for though nature . . . is the same in all places, and reason too the same; yet the climate, the age, the disposition of the people, to whom a poet writes" so affect the character of his work that any critical examination which neglects these conditions is bound to lead to false conclusions.

In adopting this line of argument Dryden may well have been influenced by Saint-Evremond, who had tried to show in some detail how the genius and the artistic standards of a people were determined by national character and climatic conditions. Similar conceptions were advanced by John Dennis in his preface to *The Impartial Critic* (1693); and one of the great functions of the eighteenth century in literary and æsthetic criticism was to develop this historical and scientific way of approach and to enrich its materials. Criticism thus became in this period more scholarly in method, and hence more catholic in outlook.

Reflection of these Diverse Elements in the Critical Writings of Addison and Pope. When account is taken of these diverse currents in the critical thought of the opening of the century, it is not surprising that individual writers, such as Dennis, Addison, and Pope, should present—sometimes within the compass of a single work—ideas derived from very different sources, and occasionally inconsistent with each other.

In the criticism of Addison neo-classic doctrine was tempered with elements of more liberal thought. He was well acquainted with the writings of Boileau, Rapin, and Saint-Evremond, and drew much from them; his critical approach to *Paradise Lost* was greatly influenced by Le Bossu, and his idea of Taste owed something to Bouhours. But his conception of the poet's moral and religious function came from the Puritan thought of Milton, and his classicism was throughout modified by the independence traditionally claimed for the English national genius. This is seen especially in his view of tragedy and in his attitude to Shakespeare (*Spectator*, Nos. 39–40, 42, 44). Again, in essays such as those on the ballads and on 'the Fairy Way of Writing,' he allowed himself to be guided by 'Taste,' without making constant reference to the precepts of classical criticism; and this freedom of outlook was doubtless encouraged by his interest in the new psychological study of genius and artistic creation which the writings of Hobbes and of Locke had inspired. The essays on 'The Pleasures of the Imagination' and on 'Taste,' which were to a large extent based on Locke's psychology, made a notable contribution to the Romantic theory of poetry.

The critical writings of Pope reveal a similar mingling of elements. The youthful *Essay on Criticism* was in part a restatement of the neo-classic and rationalist doctrine of the previous generation; but it was closely linked with the movement of 'Taste' in its view of genius and notion of criticism. Pope's prefaces to his translation of Homer and to his edition of Shakespeare were still more definitely pre-Romantic in outlook. The preface to the translation of the *Iliad*, while following traditional neo-classic lines in its account of the qualities and defects of Homer's poetry, contained a bold and vigorous championship of Genius or Imagination as the essential gift of the poet. In the preface to Shakespeare Pope endeavoured, at least in part, to view Shakespeare's drama in relation to its period, and thus provided the text for those well-known paragraphs of Johnson's preface in which he maintains that "every man's performances, to be rightly estimated, must be compared with the state of the age in which he lived and with his own particular opportunities." It is indeed by these writings, and by his essays in *The Guardian*, rather than by the *Essay on Criticism* that Pope should be judged as a critic.

THE EVOLUTION OF TASTE, 1710–60

*Enlargement of the Conception of Art, and especially of Poetry:
the Weakening of the Rules and of the Conception of the 'Kinds.'*
Under the stimulus of these new ideas of Taste and of historical
criticism a larger conception of poetry and art became current,
and the limits set to poetic expression in the name of neo-
classic formalism, or of good sense or decorum, were gradually
broken down. It was realized that Nature could not be confined
within the Rules; that the field of poetry was more complex
than the system of the classical 'kinds' suggested; that, from
the artistic standpoint, the particular or individual was as
significant as the general or universal; that sentiment was as
essential as reason in art; that other forms of civilization might
be as interesting as that of the ancient Mediterranean world;
and that the expression of Christian experience might be more
vital than the refurbishing of pagan mythology.

From this time there was, in short, a growing tendency for
the modern and the Romantic to assume equal importance
with the classical, and for genius or imagination to be exalted
above judgment or good sense. Others besides Hurd realized
what had been lost by the subjection of fancy to reason.
"What we have gotten by this revolution, you will say, is a
great deal of good sense. What we have lost, is a world of fine
fabling: the illusion of which is so grateful to the charmed
spirit." (*Letters on Chivalry*, xii.)

The new spirit showed itself simultaneously in the substance
and in the form of literature, and one of its most obvious
manifestations was in the change that came about in the conception of the 'kinds' or 'genres' which the seventeenth
century had inherited from the Renaissance. The emergence of
the novel—almost a creation of the eighteenth century—
undoubtedly played a particularly important part in helping to
destroy belief in the old notion of the fixed kinds. The novel

(and especially the realistic novel) was confessedly a new form, distinct from the classical romance and from the medieval prose tale, and as such could not be lightly dismissed. Though the earlier examples, as in Defoe, were sometimes presented as journals or memoirs, it became more and more evident, as the century proceeded, that the novel was a successful innovation, whereas some of the older literary genres, such as the epic, were falling into decay.

Several of the great works of the century, especially *Tom Jones* and *Tristram Shandy*, with their mixture of realism, mock-heroic, and miscellaneous reflections, were clear challenges to the notion of the kinds; and it is evident from Fielding's critical comments on this and other points that he was quite aware of the insufficiency of classical critical dogma.

In eighteenth-century poetry, again, there were many works which could scarcely have been classified under the old division of the kinds as set out by Sidney or Boileau. The spheres of the lyric and of reflective or elegiac verse were greatly enlarged in the period 1710–50: poems such as Thomson's *Seasons*, Dyer's *Grongar Hill*, and Young's *Night Thoughts*, while loosely related with earlier forms, were essentially new departures; and the longer lyrics of the mid-century, whether entitled 'ode' or not, exemplified an enormous variety of forms and purposes.

English writers were doubtless encouraged in their free handling of literary forms by the long tradition of independence in our literature, especially in poetry and drama. The success that our poets and dramatists had achieved in defiance of classical canons was a constant obstacle to attempts to apply rigid rules in English letters, and *The Faerie Queene*, the tragi-comedies of Beaumont and Fletcher, and the plays of Shakespeare were perpetual reminders of this tradition.

The Widening View of Literature; the Importance of the Study of Spenser and Milton. This critical independence was greatly

strengthened by the growth of the historical and textual
study of our earlier literature. Eighteenth-century critics
began the serious textual study of Chaucer, Spenser, and
Shakespeare; they instituted a scientific study of prosody; and,
partly through these studies, and partly through the general
discussions arising out of the Ancients and Moderns controversy, they began to understand more exactly than their
predecessors had done the nature of the relationship that
exists between a work of art and its period. In particular, they
came to see more clearly the differences between the 'classical'
and the 'Gothic,' and between the medieval and the modern.

The study of Milton was of special importance in this
connexion. Milton's poetry was at first regarded from the
neo-classical point of view: thus Addison explained and
defended *Paradise Lost* by reference to classical models, and Dr
Johnson, whose three essays on Milton's versification in *The
Rambler* (Nos. 86, 88, 90) contained much judicious and
well-tempered criticism, was still largely concerned, as the
essays on *Samson Agonistes* (Nos. 139, 140) also show, with
the formal criticism of Milton's poetry. The qualities that
Johnson sought in Milton were those of logical and organic
structure, consistency of tone, and clarity of expression. But
the Wartons, both father and sons, approached Milton from a
more purely poetic standpoint, and in the second half of the
century Milton's romantic qualities and the sublimity of his
imagination and of his verse-music came to be fully appreciated.

Even before the imaginative side of Milton's genius was
properly understood, however, his poetry and his view of
poetry exerted a notable influence, which in the main ran
counter to the neo-classic creed. Milton, though steeped in
classical literature and employing classical forms, had chosen
Biblical subjects for his epics and his tragedy. He had, moreover, claimed for the poet divine inspiration and a divine
mission; and this he had done not in mere imitation of classical
custom, but in a vital Christian sense. The poet was for him far

more than an artist putting into words "what oft was thought, but ne'er so well expressed"; poetic justice was:

> The inspired gift of God, rarely bestowed . . . and of power to inbreed and cherish in a great people the seeds of virtue and public civility, . . . and to celebrate in glorious and lofty hymns the throne and equipage of God's Almightiness.

The influence of Milton's poetic doctrine became naturally associated with that of the critical doctrine of 'Longinus.' Those who believed that modern poetry could find in religion its inspiration and its theme stressed the essential place of passion or enthusiasm in all true poetic experience and in all true criticism. This conception was strongly maintained by John Dennis in his *Advancement and Reformation of Modern Poetry* (1701) and *Grounds of Criticism in Poetry* (1704), and by Isaac Watts in his preface to the second edition of his *Horæ Lyricæ* (1709). For critics such as these it was Milton, rather than Shakespeare, who was the great English example of the inspired poet; and Milton's later poetry was the supreme modern illustration of that sublimity of style and thought so long associated with Homer.

These movements towards the enlargement of the sphere of literature (and especially of poetry), towards the laying of greater emphasis on inspiration and feeling, and towards more liberal methods of criticism, were greatly assisted by parallel developments in other realms of art and thought, and by the growth of æsthetic speculation.

The New Interest in Nature: Landscape Painting and the Landscape Garden. One of the most profound tendencies of the first half of the century, and one of the main sources of inspiration in Romantic poetry, was the new interest taken in the world of Nature. The origin of this was philosophic rather than literary. It may be clearly seen in the writings of Shaftesbury, one of the most influential minds in the early part of the age. Shaftesbury's passionate interest in nature and its primitive,

untamed state was in marked contrast with the fear of the wild
and uncultivated which had been characteristic of the seventeenth century. The seventeenth century had been the age of
the formal garden, the time when Thomas Burnet in his
Theory of the Earth (1681) could view the irregular formation of
this planet and of the universe as being a divine punishment
for man's original disobedience towards his Creator. Shaftesbury, on the contrary, saw Nature as 'supremely fair and
sovereignly good,' and thus provided the text for the famous
Hymn with which Thomson concluded his *Seasons*.

The Seasons (1726–30) were the most ambitious attempt in the
first half of the century to paint in verse the beauty and wonder
of the natural world; but other poets, such as Lady Winchelsea
and John Dyer, had already rediscovered its poetic value.
Later poets, such as the Wartons, Gray, and Collins, besides
noting and describing the external beauty of nature, attempted
to seize the 'atmosphere' of natural scenes, and Cowper
advanced to the suggestion of a spiritual link between nature
and man.

Painting and landscape-gardening contributed as much as
poetry to this rediscovery of the beauty of Nature and to this
perception of its spiritual values. These arts were greatly
encouraged by men of fashion and wealthy amateurs, and thus
came to occupy a central place in the culture of the period.

Interest in painting was stimulated particularly by the
practice of making the 'grand tour,' which had become a
recognized part of the education of the wealthy in the seventeenth century. Most travellers brought back prints and
engravings, and some brought original paintings by Continental masters, or copies of them. From about 1720 the number of
these to be found in English noble houses increased rapidly.

Among the works most admired in England were the
classical and idealized landscapes of the seventeenth-century
French masters Claude (le Lorrain) and Nicholas Poussin and
their imitators—partly, no doubt, because of the connexion

in subject-matter between their work and classical pastoral poetry. The paintings of the Dutch and Flemish schools were also well known. The work of the Dutch landscape artists from Rembrandt to Hobbema was characterized by the realistic presentation of natural forms, and the paintings of some of these masters, especially those of Cuyp and Ruysdael, were much esteemed. The gloomy and often sensational scenes of mountain storms, rocks, and torrents painted by Salvator Rosa made an even deeper impression on the mind of the period. Each of these landscape schools had its imitators in England, but their diverse characteristics were first gathered together in this country in the work of Richard Wilson (1714–82), the first English painter of Italian scenes and the historical link between Poussin and Constable. Wilson was one of the first British artists to attempt to put on canvas the beauty and magnificence of mountain scenery; he was equally skilful in his rendering of simple English landscape, and was a great master of the presentation of skies, of light, and of water.

Wilson and his contemporaries, George Lambert, Samuel Scott, George Barret, John Inigo Richards, Gainsborough, Joseph Wright of Derby, and John Robert Cozens, may be said to have created English landscape painting; and after about 1760 Horace Walpole could no longer have complained that, owing to the demand for Italian subjects, English painters had neglected the "ever verdant lawns, rich vales, fields of haycocks and hopgrounds" of our country, "so profusely beautiful with the amenities of nature."

The widespread interest in landscape painting reacted on the sister-art of garden-design. At the Restoration Charles II and his court had brought from France the taste for grand and extensive schemes, in which radiating avenues of trees, or long straight canals, formed the basic plan, and in which fountains and statues provided the main ornaments. Hampton Court, Badminton Park, and Wrest Park (Bedfordshire) were in a large degree imitative of Le Nôtre's laying-out of the grounds of Versailles. With the accession of William III some of the elements of the Dutch garden had been incorporated into the design of the parterres and cultivated portions of these gardens: thick hedges of clipped yew or alleys of pleached lime or beech were used to divide the flower-gardens, which were themselves laid out in symmetrical and geometrical patterns. At the same time individual trees and shrubs were cut into geometrical shapes or into the form of birds and animals— the art of 'topiary.'

But before the close of the reign of Anne this artificial manner of gardening was already being challenged. Shaftes-bury's depreciatory remarks on formal gardens and artificial labyrinths were followed by the attacks of Addison and Pope on topiary art and on excessive symmetry in the planning of gardens. Addison stressed particularly the desirability of allowing trees and shrubs to develop naturally, and thought that the garden ought to appear to be a part of the surrounding landscape. From the time of Stephen Switzer (? 1682–1745), who was designing gardens in the reigns of George I and George II, these ideas were applied in the making of new gardens and in the remodelling of old ones; and in the middle decades of the century the work of Charles Bridgeman (died 1738) and of Lancelot ("Capability") Brown (1715–83) continued this trend.

Refinements in the theory and practice of landscape garden-ing followed quickly on the development of landscape painting. "All gardening is landscape painting," said Pope. "I think," said Shenstone, "the landscape painter is the gardener's best designer." Shenstone, Mason, and Whateley all stressed the view that design in gardening ought to imitate the 'occult balance' and emotional unity achieved by the masters of landscape in painting.

Although certain fashionable crazes, such as the building of grottoes and Gothic hermitages, were allowed to invade the 'natural' garden, this rediscovery of Nature and reaction against seventeenth-century formalism was still a most important æsthetic and spiritual development.

The Gothic. The growth of the taste for natural and landscape gardens was also closely linked with reactions against the more extreme forms of classicism in architecture. The Queen Anne period saw the climax of the extravagant and aristocratic building exemplified in the work of Sir John Vanbrugh (1666–1726) at Blenheim Palace, Seaton Delaval, and Castle Howard; but this vogue was a divergence from the national tradition, and it is not surprising that it soon became the object of attacks by satirists and social critics. It was not this massive and flamboyant style, but rather the academic Palladian style sponsored by Burlington which remained until the end of the century the dominant mode of building for the houses of the wealthy and for public purposes. It was in this 'correct' style that Kent (1684–1748) worked, designing magnificent buildings such as Holkham (Norfolk), Rousham (Oxfordshire), the Horse Guards in Whitehall, or Worcester Lodge at Badminton. But the Palladian style, in spite of its 'correctness,' was regarded as slightly alien in England, and as an imitative rather than an original art; it was this feeling that inspired Pope's lines addressed to Burlington in the IVth Epistle of the *Moral Essays*:

> You show us, Rome was glorious, not profuse,
> And pompous buildings once were things of use,
> Yet shall (my Lord) your just, your noble rules,
> Fill half the land with imitating fools;
> Who random drawings from your sheets shall take,
> And of one beauty many blunders make;
> Load some vain church with old theatric state,
> Turn arcs of triumph to a garden-gate;
> Reverse your ornaments, and hang them all
> On some patch'd dog-hole ek'd with ends of wall;
> Then clap four slices of Pilaster on't,

That, lac'd with bits of rustic, makes a front.
Shall call the winds through long arcades to roar,
Proud to catch cold at a Venetian door;
Conscious they act a true Palladian part,
And, if they starve, they starve by rules of art.

As applied to the building of ordinary houses and smaller public buildings in both town and country, the imposed Roman architecture underwent considerable modification by native traditions. Nor did it escape the effects of other influences. In the middle of the century the treatment of interior design and ornament was much affected by the style of decoration known as 'Rococo,' which was introduced from France at this time, and was characterized by the graceful and varied use of delicate motifs, of asymmetry, and of curves and flowing lines. This movement linked naturally, if unexpectedly, with the teaching of the painter Hogarth, who, in his *Analysis of Beauty* (1753), set out to show that the curved or undulating line (and not the straight line or circle as the classicists had maintained) was the most beautiful, and that beauty consisted, not in unity or 'uniformity in variety,' but rather in intricacy or continuity in variety.

In interior design the rococo fashion was chiefly revealed in the increasingly elaborate carving that filled mantelpieces and door-cases, and in the intricate plasterwork with which ceilings and friezes were covered. The taste for rococo also had a profound effect on the design of furniture and domestic appointments. Chippendale furniture and Chelsea porcelain were in a large measure products of this movement.

There was a natural bond between the development of rococo and the revival of interest in Gothic architecture which dated from quite early in the eighteenth century. The Gothic tradition had never really died out in the provinces, even though it had been eclipsed by classical influences in London. The Society of Arts, founded in London in 1707, and similar societies in the provinces, began to interest themselves in the preservation of medieval buildings, monuments, and *objets d'art*. Many individual writers and topographers, of whom Defoe is now the best known, contributed to this end, and extolled the beauty of the Gothic cathedrals of York, Lincoln, and Lichfield. It should be noted that this true enthusiasm for medieval art preceded the fashionable building of ruins, grottoes, and sham Gothic towers in great estates, and that it was manifestly active for several decades before Horace Walpole began to make his famous collection of Gothic curiosities and to gothicize his home at Strawberry Hill.

In these early years the interest taken in Gothic, even by a man of Horace Walpole's standing, was largely uncritical and uninstructed. Gothic architecture was vaguely associated with the period of the Saxon kingdom and the Danish invasions of England; and the historical relationship between the Norman, Early English, Decorated, and Perpendicular periods was not appreciated. The poet Gray was the first to understand the true historical setting of Gothic architecture and to claim that medieval Gothic reached the peak of its achievement in the middle of the fourteenth century.

It must indeed be admitted that the eighteenth-century taste for Gothic architecture was more sentimental than artistic in basis. The artificial Gothic ruins, such as the ruined castle designed by Sanderson Miller at Hagley, the Gothic grottoes and hermitages, and even buildings such as the Great Hall at Lacock Abbey, Wiltshire, met an emotional rather than an artistic need, and an architect such as Batty Langley (1696–1751), who had some real appreciation of the principles of Gothic design, was frequently content to apply his technical knowledge to what seem to us very absurd ends.

It is not untrue to say, in fact, that the eighteenth-century Gothic revival, in contrast to Romanticism in literature, never became truly integrated with the social life of the age. Thus, while it was a rival, it never usurped the well-established position of the classical styles in this period. It is not without

C

significance that James Wyatt, the architect both of the sham-Gothic Ashridge and of the long since vanished Fonthill Abbey, was even more famous as the designer of buildings conceived in a graceful and simplified classical manner. Good examples of this work, in which he rivalled Robert Adam, are the interiors of Heveningham Hall, Suffolk, or of Heaton Park, Manchester.

Oriental Influences. While antiquaries and tourists were thus rediscovering English medieval art, a new field of imaginative interest was being opened up through increased communication with the Far East. A steady development of trade with India, Siam, China, and Japan had taken place in the sixteenth and seventeenth centuries; and Oriental porcelain, textiles, lacquer work, furniture, and wall-papers were extremely popular in Western Europe during the period 1690–1770. Books of Eastern travel and descriptions of the countries and customs of the East had been extensively read throughout the seventeenth century, and left their mark on the literature of the succeeding age, both in works of fiction or satire, such as *Gulliver's Travels,* and in such writings as Goldsmith's *Citizen of the World,* in which idealized conceptions of Oriental (especially Chinese) culture provided a basis for criticism of the Western world. The use of Oriental motives was, however, less important in literature than in other fields of art. It was the craze for Indian cotton and chintzes, and for Chinese lacquer goods, furniture, and wall-papers, that brought home to the English public the freedom, intricacy, and variety of Eastern art; and although patriots and economists expressed fears for the security of the home wool trade, and philosophers and essayists criticized the taste for Eastern art as a betrayal of our classical heritage, the nation was not to be denied the delight and imaginative freedom which were embodied in these exotic forms.

Here was a new and powerful ally of the Gothic, and of naturalism; so that the formalism of classical and neo-classical styles in architecture and decoration was henceforth subject to opposition from three directions at once.

Æsthetic and Literary Theory, 1710–60. (*a*) *The Analysis of Imagination.* Highly significant developments took place in the first half of the eighteenth century in æsthetic and literary theory. The period inherited from the preceding age the desire to analyse the nature of artistic creation, and attempted to explain the working of imagination or fancy, the significance of taste and its relation to reason, the nature of genius, and the relationship between the claims of genius and the authority of the Rules. These speculations advanced hand in hand with a growing recognition of the distinction between æsthetic experience and perceptions of truth, goodness, or utility—between man's feeling for beauty and his sense of reason.

The nature of the imagination as a creative faculty, and as a power of the mind distinct from memory or reason, had been clearly recognized by Bacon; but later seventeenth-century psychologists had, as has been shown above, tended to explain artistic creation primarily in terms of reason, and to lay stress on judgment rather than on fantasy. Thus Hobbes had regarded the poetic faculty as a union of fancy (or wit) and judgment (or reason) in which judgment was the controlling power. He had thought of imagination as a purely subordinate faculty which discovered effects of novelty and played a certain part in the association of ideas.

Dryden's view of poetic creation had, with some differences in terminology, been mainly based on that of Hobbes; but Addison, although he adopted the empiricism of Locke, inaugurated a more profound treatment of the subject. He saw that imagination was not to be subordinated to understanding, and realized that it linked together the world of the intellect and that of the senses. In dealing with what he called the 'secondary pleasures' of imagination, he demonstrated the inventive or idealizing power of this faculty, and in his essay on the 'fairy way of writing' gave further illustrations of it in its form of fantasy. He showed also that the rôle of imagination was not confined to the world of art, and that this faculty played an important part in other spheres of intellectual creation, such as history and science. The psychologists of the mid-century, Hume and Hartley, while seeking to explain imaginative processes as far as possible through the theory of the association of ideas, never denied this inventive power of imagination.

(b) The Question of a Standard of Taste, and the Idea of Genius; 'Relativity' of Judgment. The analysis of the nature of the imagination had immediate repercussions on current views about genius and taste, and especially about the reality of a 'standard of taste.' In the age of Dryden, when an attempt had been made to develop a practice of reasoned criticism, claims had naturally been made by critics for the existence of such a standard of artistic judgment, and writers on æsthetic questions followed suit. Shaftesbury and Bishop Berkeley believed that the existence of a standard of taste followed logically from the universal nature of the human sense of beauty, and Reynolds later sought to link this conception with his theory of ideal beauty and of the 'grand style.'

But it was not the classical tenet of a standard of taste or judgment which was to prevail. The main tendency of the century was towards the idea of 'relativity' in æsthetic appreciation. Literary critics and writers on æsthetics came more and more to favour the view already adopted by Hobbes, by Dennis, and by Pope in the preface to his edition of Shakespeare, that ideas of beauty or artistic excellence were always in part determined by factors of history, climate, and national temperament, and by the inexplicable nature of individual genius. Thus Addison, while showing that taste might be improved by study, and hence that it might be related with tradition, also recognized that it incorporated an innate or original element, and admitted that, in the last resort, genius, a power above all rules, was the essential factor in artistic creation.

Burke made an even more comprehensive analysis of the conception of taste. He was prepared to admit that the common nature of men's minds caused them to make similar æsthetic judgments, but pointed out that differences existed in the intensity and direction of the taste of different persons. He saw, too, that taste, while not a mere instinct, was not a separate faculty of the mind, but depended on the harmonious working of sensibility, judgment, and imagination. This clear relating of terms was long overdue.

A similar balancing of evidence marked Hume's treatment of the subject in his essay "Of the Standard of Taste" (1757), and from about this time, as a result of the gradual relinquishing of the Rules and of classical standards, the validity of individual taste and the independence of imaginative genius were clearly recognized. Young's famous letter to Samuel Richardson *Conjectures on Original Composition* (1759) threw out a bold challenge for this liberal and Romantic conception of genius, and Alexander Gerard's treatise of 1774 made the first systematic analysis of it.

The new doctrine most readily secured recognition from those writers who had adopted the historical method of criticism, and especially from the critics of major authors such as Shakespeare and Spenser. The value attributed to genius as 'the master workman' forced men of letters to consider more completely and more carefully the nature and merit of earlier works of literature which had not sprung from the classical tradition. This historical research, like the theory which supported it, became a vital element in the growth of the Romantic movement in literature.

The examination of these topics shows very clearly the perfectly natural and gradual development of critical thought in this period. On all the questions of taste, of genius, and of the Rules, there was a slow evolution of thought through the first half of the century, and no definite break between classical and modern theory.

(c) *The Theory of Beauty; Importance of Burke's "Of the Sublime and Beautiful."* The æsthetic theory of the century falls into no very clearly cut pattern. In the early years the influence of Platonic conceptions was strong in writers such as Shaftesbury and Berkeley; and in Britain, as in France, spiritual and moral theories of beauty predominated. Although it would be incorrect to suggest that there was a well-defined school of thought on this subject, the chief British writers of this time —Shaftesbury, Hutcheson, and Berkeley—were agreed that beauty lay, not in the physical qualities of objects, but 'in the eye of the beholder.' An object or action is recognized as beautiful when it makes a particular kind of appeal to the mind of man, and beauty is the soul-satisfying harmony set up between man's innate sense of beauty and objects of sense, or, equally, actions and ideas—for to the thinkers of this school man's sense of beauty is stirred not only by objects belonging to the physical world but also by human actions and ideas. Beauty may be moral or intellectual as well as physical.

None of the early writers worked out a complete or consistent theory. Spence, while stressing the pre-eminence of moral beauty, attempted to analyse the beauty of the human form into its physical elements. Hutcheson was drawn from his idealistic theory into a discussion of beauty as the combination of uniformity and variety. The weakness of the æsthetic theory of the whole group, as their critics were quick to realize, was that it left beauty itself undefined; beauty remained the *je ne sais quoi*.

The natural reaction against these abstract speculations came in the attack made on the problem from the empirical side. Hume, Burke, and Hogarth begin from the assumption that beauty is a quality residing in objects themselves and capable of analysis. The pleasurable emotion aroused in us by certain objects is conceived as being produced by certain identifiable shapes, movements, colours, or sounds; while other material forms produce the opposite effect of pain or a sense of deformity. In these experiences custom and associations, derived either from individual experience or from the history of the race, have come to play a large part, so that the analysis of beauty is rarely straightforward; but there is among men a broad agreement that certain physical and moral qualities are beautiful, or ugly, or sublime, or ridiculous; and the theory of beauty can thus become a subject of physiological and psychological study.

The danger of concentration on this empirical æsthetic was that the spiritual and moral values associated with our perception of beauty or sublimity might be disregarded. But there is little doubt that the pursuit of these empirical and psychological lines of study formed the most important contribution of the eighteenth century to this subject.

THE SECOND HALF OF THE CENTURY

The Persistence of the Classical Tradition in Art and in Literary and Æsthetic Theory: Dr Johnson, Robert Adam, Sir Joshua Reynolds. Except in the case of a Burke or a Kames, however, the results of these æsthetic and psychological speculations had not, by 1760, been incorporated into critical theory. Classical dogma persisted, indeed, especially in academic circles, throughout the latter half of the century and into the Romantic period. For Blair in 1783, as for Hume a generation earlier, Shakespeare was "deficient in just taste, and altogether unassisted by knowledge of art"; and William Richardson, who gave us our earliest full-length analysis of Macbeth and Hamlet (1774), Richard III and King Lear (1784), could also write a neo-classical essay "On the Faults of Shakespeare." The notion of the fixed 'kinds' remained powerful through the century, in spite of opposition, and so did the idea of readily determined values in art. Thus Goldsmith published in the *Literary Magazine* for January 1758 "A Poetical Scale," in which twenty-nine English poets were graded according to the merits of their genius, judgment, learning, and versification.

More direct attacks on Romanticism in literature or art were numerous throughout the period, and sometimes achieved a useful purpose in checking absurdities or excesses. Thus writers in periodicals such as *The World* (1753–56) satirized the excesses of Gothicism, of Orientalism, and of Romantic gardening, basing their attacks sometimes on the claims of good sense, sometimes on the value of the classical tradition. Occasionally, on the other hand, classical theory was invoked for the defence of 'pre-Romantic' poetry: for example, Blair praised Macpherson's *Ossian* in much the same spirit as Addison defended *Paradise Lost*, and tried to show that *Fingal* and *Temora* were epic poems constructed on Aristotelian principles and possessing the unity of a central action elaborated with subordinate episodes.

For the most valuable classical criticism of the mid-century we must, of course, turn to Dr Johnson.

It is true that Johnson's critical writing was sometimes conservative and that he had only a limited appreciation of some of the new movements in the culture of his time. His mind—except in the political sphere—tended to be governed by reason and morality rather than by imagination and sentiment. He was trained in the neo-classic school, and was well versed in classical and Renaissance Latin literature. He had little interest in nature, and no eye for scenery. He was not gifted with an ear for music, or for the subtleties of verse-harmony, and continued to regard the strict versification of Dryden and Pope, the masters of his early years, as the perfection of poetic expression. But, on the other hand, Johnson's critical writings were characterized by good sense, appreciation of form and structure, and broad humanity of outlook. His reason was too vigorous, his insight too brilliant, to be crushed by rule or tradition. It was these positive qualities that gave the preface to his edition of Shakespeare a value unequalled in the Shakespeare criticism of the age.

At some points, indeed, Johnson came into unconscious sympathy with trends of thought that were to lead towards Romanticism. As early as *The Rambler*, No. 156 (1745), he denied the possibility of fixing limits for the imagination, and (as in the later preface) defended Shakespeare's use of tragi-comedy and his disregard of the unities of time and place. His devotion to the Augustans did not prevent him from admiring Milton's *L'Allegro* and Gray's *Elegy*, or from having a taste for medieval romances.

The *Discourses* delivered by Sir Joshua Reynolds, as President of the Royal Academy, between 1769 (the year of its opening) and 1790, were in some ways a more direct expression of the classical ideals of art. Reynolds looked back to Michelangelo and Raphael, the giants of the Italian Renaissance, as the greatest masters in his art, and based his art teaching on classical principles. It was his aim to "establish the rules and principles" of painting, and he held firmly that some of the exaggerated notions of genius which were current in his day were false and absurd. He maintained that, while it might be true that artistic excellence could only arise from natural or innate gifts, such natural talents demanded intellectual support and constant study for their development. He refused to conceive of artistic beauty as a shifting *je ne sais quoi*; beauty was for him the essential or ideal truth implied in nature, a truth capable of being seized by the imagination of the artist and by the taste of the enlightened spectator. Reynolds's repeated declarations that the aim of art was to represent this ideal beauty, and that a standard of artistic truth and of taste really existed, undoubtedly did much to strengthen the currency of classical theory in the latter part of the century, even though his own theory of beauty and his view of the history of painting were in reality much more complex and more modern in tendency.

It was, however, in architecture, sculpture, and the decorative arts that the classical tradition was most clearly shown; and the notable increases that were made at this time in the knowledge of ancient Greek and Roman architecture and sculpture helped to strengthen the classical position. Scientific excavations had been steadily pursued at Herculaneum and Pompeii in the forties and fifties; and the Society of Dilettanti (founded in London in 1732) gave support to a number of journeys made in the Mediterranean countries, and also into Asia Minor, to discover further remains of ancient Greek and Roman life. The publication of accounts of these expeditions, and of drawings of hitherto unknown buildings and works of art, had a great effect both on classical learning and on the plastic and decorative arts. In particular, these discoveries brought to light aspects of classical architecture which had not been revealed by the study of Vitruvius or seen in ruined remains of Roman public buildings: in the words of Horace Walpole, "The discoveries at Herculaneum testify that a light and fantastic architecture of a very Indian air makes a common decoration of private apartments" in Græco-Roman dwellings. Impulses derived from this new learning were clearly seen in the domestic architecture of the Adam brothers, the furniture of Hepplewhite and Sheraton, and the designs of Josiah Wedgwood.

The Adam brothers were conscious rebels against the Palladian tradition. In the hands of Robert Adam (1728–92), the best-known of the four brothers, all the elements of the interior of the house became objects of rich decoration, and were brought into artistic unity. Ceilings and friezes were not only filled with intricate and delicate plasterwork, but were also richly coloured. Mirrors and gilding, pillars and statues, contributed to the richness of the walls. Chimney-pieces, staircase balustrades, grates, and fenders (and even exterior railings) became elaborate works of art. Carpets and furniture—much of this being executed by Chippendale— were designed to harmonize with the decoration of the rooms themselves.

In all this art there was manifested a new grace and delicacy of effect, in which the liveliness of Oriental and rococo influences seemed at length to be blended with classical grace and proportion.

Romantic Elements in Literary Criticism in the Second Half of the Century: the Growth of Literary History; Importance of the Work of Thomas Warton and of Bishop Hurd. The latter part of the eighteenth century was, in the critical field, a period of consolidation, rather than of radical changes of thought such as had occurred in the years 1710–60; its chief work was to deepen the lines of study inaugurated in the earlier years. The critical and textual study of our older poets, particularly of Chaucer, Spenser, Shakespeare, and Milton, was advanced; the fields of literary history and of prosody were further explored, especially with reference to the medieval and Elizabethan periods; and public interest in critical questions was widened. Poets such as Shenstone and William Mason, and essayists like Vicesimus Knox, sought to popularize ideas on imagination and taste, as Pope and Akenside had done in the previous generation.

The main tendency of the literature of the last third of the century was towards Romanticism. Bolder claims were made for the pre-eminence of genius or imagination in poetic creation, while excellence of imitation and reference to the Rules came to be despised as of little value. In these respects the movement of literature, though running counter to that of architecture and decorative art, was clearly in harmony with the deeper philosophic and social tendencies of the age.

The outstanding critical development of this time was the rise in importance of historical criticism and of literary history.

The relationship between literary criticism and the study of history had been clearly perceived in the Shakespeare criticism of the early years of the century; but by 1765, the year of Johnson's preface, the real significance of such historical considerations had become much more fully and more widely recognized.

Moreover, the field of literature calling for study had been greatly enlarged. Antiquarian study, which had been carried on spasmodically from Elizabethan times, began to yield a much richer harvest in the eighteenth century. Thomas Carte, in his *General History of England* (1747), showed an interest in Celtic antiquities; and in the fifties Gray made prolonged researches into the history and literature of medieval Europe and into the earlier literature and civilization of Wales and Scandinavia. Although *The Bard* and the 'Norse fragments' were the only published results of his detailed studies, his example doubtless served to stimulate interest in these little-known realms. Celtic studies were at this time being taken up in Oxford, where the Clarendon Press published in 1764 the Rev. Evan Evans's *Some Specimens of the Poetry of the Antient Welsh Bards, translated into English*. Collins's *Ode on the Popular Superstitions of the Highlands*, written in 1749, revealed a similar interest in Gaelic folklore; and Macpherson's first fragments of *Ossian* were received with great enthusiasm in 1760. Percy's *Reliques of Ancient English Poetry* (1765)—in the collection of which Shenstone had played some part—was greeted with genuine, if more temperate, appreciation; and it is noteworthy that Percy attempted, in the scholarly essays interspersed in his anthology, to give some of the historical background necessary for the proper understanding of the poems.

The work of two critics in particular, Thomas Warton and Bishop Hurd, contributed to the encouragement of a more general interest in these wider fields of literary history.

Warton's earlier critical writings, his essays in *The Adventurer* on Greek literature, on the poetry of the Old Testament, on Shakespeare and Milton, and his *Observations on the Faerie Queene of Spenser* (1754) played, like his poetry, an important part in the development of pre-Romanticism in England. The *Observations on the Faerie Queene* were especially significant. Earlier critics, such as John Hughes, had tried to indicate the real nature of Spenser's poetry and the spirit in which his work should be judged; Addison had vindicated the 'fairy way of writing'; and Shakespeare critics from Pope onward had pointed to the essential difference between the Greek, or heroic, and the medieval, or Gothic, strains in European literature; but Warton's criticism of Spenser was more penetrating and more complete than any of these earlier studies. Warton had a firmer sense than any of his predecessors of the historical evolution of poetry, and showed that *The Faerie Queene*, a work of Gothic or Romantic origin, could not be judged by classical precepts, but had to be viewed in the light of a study of the social character and literary heritage of the Elizabethan age.

Hurd's reputation as a critic was established by his edition (1753) of Horace's Epistles to the Pisones and to Augustus, with its Commentary and dissertations "On the Provinces of the Several Species of Dramatic Poetry," and "On Poetical Imitation." These essays, like Hurd's earlier study of Addison, were founded on neo-classic principles, but were clearly marked by the advancing historical outlook of the century, for Hurd was aware that works of modern literature were necessarily differentiated by their historical circumstances from those of classical antiquity. Hurd had also the distinction of being the first eighteenth-century critic to realize fully the greatness of Elizabethan literature, and its worthiness to be compared with that of the Augustan period.

His finest criticism is contained in the *Letters on Chivalry and Romance*, published in 1762 to illustrate the third of his *Moral and Political Dialogues*, that entitled "On the Golden Age of

Queen Elizabeth." No previous writer had appreciated so fully the true nature of the Romantic poetry of Ariosto and Tasso, and its influence on Spenser and Milton. No other writer, with the exception of Young, had made such bold claims for invention and for *poetical* truth as opposed to the so-called "truth of Nature."

Hurd's classical scholarship and his position in the society of his day no doubt lent weight to his arguments, and helped to encourage a taste for Romantic literature; but, as he was confessedly no medieval scholar, it fell to others (and particularly to Warton) to develop the study of literary history for which the *Letters* had emphasized the need.

Warton's major work, the unfinished *History of English Poetry from the close of the Eleventh to the commencement of the Eighteenth Century* (1774–78), in which the unfulfilled intentions of Pope and Gray were partly incorporated, illustrated these principles of historical criticism on a wider scale, and laid a sure foundation for the work of the nineteenth century in literary history. This was the first history of literature to be conceived on fairly strict chronological lines, and to deal with literature itself, rather than with biography or gossip. It is true that Warton had little philological learning, but his *History* revealed an extensive knowledge of medieval and Renaissance literature, in Latin, English, French, and Italian, together with a lively interest in history, mythology, and folk-lore. This work was of fundamental importance in dealing a final blow to the neo-classic belief that English poetry (and especially its versification) had its true beginning in Waller and Denham—a notion reflected in Pope's *Essay on Criticism* and expressed in a more preposterous form in one of Addison's earliest writings, the *Account of the Greatest English Poets*.

The Romantic Interest in Natural Scenery and its Expression in Literature. Other philosophic and cultural movements accompanied and stimulated this enlargement of the field of literary appreciation and literary criticism. The mental horizon of educated people was being extended in a geographical as well as in a historical sense. From the middle of the century a steadily increasing interest was shown in travel, both at home and abroad, and the practice of making the Continental 'grand tour' persisted as a recognized part of aristocratic education until the outbreak of the French Revolution. At home, as we have seen, topographers and archæologists such as Defoe and William Stukeley had helped to arouse enthusiastic admiration for the beauties of our Gothic churches and cathedrals, and in the second half of the century improved roads, increased commerce, and the spread of education led the public to take a more lively interest in other parts of the country than their own, an interest extending even to the wild and mountainous regions of North Wales, the Lake District, and the Scottish Highlands.

The Romantic feeling for mountain scenery appeared first in Gray, whose early enthusiasm for the Alps was matched by his sensitive and lyrical descriptions of the Lakes. Numerous travellers in the fifties and sixties attempted to describe the beauty of the Lake District, of Wales, and of the Irish lakes, especially Killarney. By the seventies interest in these mountain regions had become universal, and the search for the 'picturesque' prevailed. Bath, Tunbridge Wells, and other spas began to lose their position as centres of fashionable travel, and tours to more distant and picturesque parts of the country became popular. Books of travel and topography now included descriptions of scenery as well as of monuments and buildings. The editor of the eighth edition (1778) of Defoe's *Tour of Great Britain* sought to meet the taste of the time by greatly increasing the amount of scenic description in the work.

There is no doubt that part of the startling success of Macpherson's *Ossian* was due to its readers' ready appreciation of the romantic and sublime scenes of nature presented in these poems; and this interest was also intimately related with the rise of the 'tale of terror.' The earlier 'Gothic romances,' such as Horace Walpole's *Castle of Otranto*, had derived their main inspiration from medievalism, but in the tale of terror, and especially in such examples as Mrs Radcliffe's *Sicilian Romance* (1790) and *Mysteries of Udolpho* (1794), natural description and the evocation of the mood of landscape were vital elements which contributed greatly to the emotional appeal of the work. Mrs Radcliffe has been appropriately called 'the Salvator Rosa of the English novel.'

Æsthetic Philosophy in the Period 1760–1800. The world of nature also became, in the later eighteenth century, the subject of more exact and detailed æsthetic consideration, and its sublimity began to be distinguished from its beauty. Its wild and solemn effects had, indeed, from the time of Boileau's commentary on 'Longinus' (1694) been used as illustrations of the 'sublime' in writing; but Burke's treatise attempted a more methodical classification of the sources of the sublime in nature, and succeeding writers continued the elaboration of this branch of æsthetic study.

At the same time the 'picturesque' became a topic of frequent discussion, and was admitted as an æsthetic category alongside beauty, grace, and sublimity. Much material for the illustration of the nature of the picturesque was provided in the writings on scenery and landscape gardening of the Rev. William Gilpin, though it was Uvedale Price who contributed most to the theoretical consideration of the subject.

In this second half of the century æsthetic theory came more and more to attract the attention of philosophers and psychologists. The formal studies of Hartley and Reid offer a marked contrast to the somewhat general and enthusiastic writings of Shaftesbury or Spence. There was still, indeed, in the æsthetic of this period a good deal of platitude, repetition, and plagiarism, and some sketchily founded philosophy. Some writers, especially the Scottish professors Gerard, Blair, and

Beattie, made the mistake of attempting to treat their subject in too comprehensive a fashion; but their work of synthesis and popularization had its value, and such essays as Gerard's *Essay on Taste* and *Essay on Genius*, if not highly original, are excellent summaries of the critical and æsthetic outlook of the time. In their own day such writings helped to co-ordinate and stabilize speculation on these subjects.

Perhaps the most influential contribution of the later years of the century was Alison's *Essay on Taste* (1790; enlarged in the second edition of 1810). Alison's explanation of beauty in terms of 'expression' and 'association' may now appear completely false; but his book was of service in working out more completely a doctrine which had been vaguely in the air for the best part of the century. Moreover, by concentrating attention on the effect of beauty on the emotions of the individual, Alison strengthened opposition to lingering notions of beauty as absolute or objective, and to beliefs in critical theories based on *a priori* principles.

CONCLUSION

The critical output of the eighteenth century as a whole was large, and many of the essays produced, especially those written for the periodicals, have no permanent value, though they served to diffuse ideas of taste and criticism among a wider public. The best of the critical writing of the time, however, had the great merit of springing from a genuine enthusiasm for works of art, and from a desire to enlarge the field of æsthetic pleasure or to understand æsthetic experience more fully. The century never lost sight of the supreme importance of the artist. There was, indeed, in the eighteenth century a certain amount of dilettantism: this was the day of the elegant amateur—but the age was not afflicted to the same extent as the modern world by devotion to professional criticism for its

D

own sake. The poet Gray was a very learned man, even by our standards, but his chief ambition was to be considered a gentleman. Throughout the period, contempt was constantly expressed for critics who adopted a niggling or pedantic attitude to contemporary artistic production; the 'mere critic' was always held in suspicion.

On the other hand, by the latter part of the century serious and philosophic criticism had won a secure place for itself in the cultural hierarchy. Whereas Swift, no mean critic in himself, had satirized literary criticism, and Addison had almost apologized for introducing critical essays into the polite sphere of *The Spectator*, writers such as Burke and Lord Kames regarded criticism as both a cultural diversion and a serious intellectual exercise. Warton went even further in stressing the social and civilizing force of this branch of learning.

A study of the literary and æsthetic criticism of the eighteenth century shows how vitally the different arts were linked together in this period. The interactions of poetry, painting, and landscape gardening were particularly important, and fruitful parallels were drawn between these arts in the critical field. The achievements of one art were frequently illumined and made more comprehensible in the light of another. Hence it is not surprising that many of the men of letters of the time, men such as Pope, Horace Walpole, Gray, and Shenstone, were skilled amateurs in a variety of other arts and branches of learning, from music and the study of medals to interior decoration and garden-design.

The story of the art and culture of this age also illustrates the unity and balance of eighteenth-century civilization in England. The period from the reign of Anne to the French Revolution was a time of stabilized intellectual and cultural development. There were, indeed, revolutions and counter-revolutions in taste, but underlying these changes was a solid foundation of reason and a sense of order and security.

Literary students, viewing the progress of the age in terms

of poetry, have perhaps tended to regard this period too much from the standpoint of the later Romantic movement, and thus have come to think of the eighteenth century as purely neo-classic in its first half, and exclusively pre-Romantic in its second. But to imagine such a 'geological fault' in the middle of the century is to falsify the whole picture. Pope was not a purely neo-classic figure, while the Wartons, Gray, Goldsmith, Hurd, or Cowper would not have allowed themselves to be called 'Romantics.'

In the æsthetic, as in the social, industrial, and political fields, the thought and productivity of the age were—until the political events of 1789 and the more acute phase of the Industrial Revolution—marked by continuity and slow evolution. In all departments there was indeed an enrichment of available materials, a deepening of spiritual perception, a transition from rationalism to romanticism. Poetry reflected most sensitively the changing spirit of the times, but in poetry, as in most forms of art, the century retained what was essentially useful in the practice of the neo-classic period, modifying and enlarging its material to suit the needs of the time. It embodied new influences, and eliminated what was purely abstract or formalistic in the theory it had inherited. Thus in architecture the Gothic excesses and Oriental exoticism of the middle years of the century were no longer in vogue at its end, but the dominant classical style had been modified alike by the Rococo movement and the new discoveries made in Greek art, and had achieved richer artistic effects than the more formal Palladianism of the earlier period.

As the century proceeded the analysis of beauty was slowly disengaged from moral philosophy and more closely linked with the study of the particular qualities and provinces of the various arts. The field of research was widened by the recognition of other æsthetic categories alongside the beautiful —namely, the sublime and the picturesque. In this way much of the foundation was laid for the work of the great German æsthetic philosophers, Lessing and Kant, and for nineteenth-century æsthetic writings such as Ruskin's *Modern Painters*.

At the same time, in the theory of literary creation the consideration of the relationship between judgment and genius focused attention on the central importance of the study of imagination; and there was a steady development of thought on this subject from Addison's essays 'On the Pleasures of Imagination,' through the writings of Burke and Reynolds, to the Romantic theory (most fully expressed by Coleridge) of the harmony of the mental faculties in artistic creation.

The achievement of the period in literary criticism itself was of great significance. In this, as in other fields of culture, the century inherited the rich harvest of Renaissance thought, and in its turn became the source of the main movements of the succeeding age. In its growing regard for exact textual study (especially of Shakespeare), in its careful analysis of individual works, in the development of the critical biography (as in Johnson's *Lives*), and in the inauguration of the true historical study of literature (as in Warton's *History*), it laid the foundations of nineteenth-century criticism and determined the chief methods of its literary study.

SELECTED TEXTS

I. *THE NEO-CLASSIC TRADITION*

ALEXANDER POPE (1688–1744): from *An Essay on Criticism*
(1709)

The Poet and Classical Rules

    First follow NATURE, and your judgment frame
By her just standard, which is still the same:
Unerring Nature, still divinely bright,
One clear, unchang'd, and universal light,
Life, force and beauty, must to all impart,
At once the source, and end, and test of art. . . .
Some, to whom Heav'n in wit has been profuse,
Want as much more, to turn it to its use;
For wit and judgment often are at strife,
Tho' meant each other's aid, like man and wife.
'Tis more to guide, than spur tne Muse's steed;
Restrain his fury, than provoke his speed;
The winged courser, like a gen'rous horse,s
Shows most true mettle when you check hi course.
    Those RULES of old discover'd, not deviz'd,
Are Nature still, but Nature methodiz'd;
Nature, like liberty, is but restrain'd
By the same laws which first herself ordain'd.
    Hear how learn'd Greece her useful rules indites,
When to repress, and when indulge our flights:
High on Parnassus' top her sons she show'd,

And pointed out those arduous paths they trod;
Held from afar, aloft, th' immortal prize,
And urg'd the rest by equal steps to rise.
Just precepts thus from great examples giv'n,
She drew from them what they deriv'd from Heav'n.
The gen'rous critic fann'd the poet's fire,
And taught the world, with reason to admire.

.   .   .   .   .

You then whose judgment the right course would steer,
Know well each ANCIENT's proper character;
His fable, subject, scope in ev'ry page;
Religion, country, genius of his age:
Without all these at once before your eyes,
Cavil you may, but never criticize.
Be Homer's works your study and delight,
Read them by day, and meditate by night.
Thence form your judgment, thence your maxims bring,
And trace the Muses upward to their spring;
Still with itself compar'd, his text peruse;
And let your comment be the Mantuan muse.
When first young Maro in his boundless mind
A work t'outlast immortal Rome design'd,
Perhaps he seem'd above the critic's law,
And but from Nature's fountains scorn'd to draw:
But when t'examine ev'ry part he came,
Nature and Homer were, he found, the same.
Convinc'd, amaz'd, he checks the bold design;
And Rules as strict his labour'd work confine,
As if the Stagyrite o'erlook'd each line.
Learn hence for Ancient Rules a just esteem;
To copy Nature is to copy them.

(lines 68–140)

Lord Shaftesbury (1671–1713): from *Characteristics* (1711)

Excellence in Taste to be acquired only by Study of the Classics

One who aspires to the character of a man of breeding and politeness is careful to form his judgment of arts and sciences upon right models of perfection. If he travels to Rome, he inquires which are the truest pieces of architecture, the best remains of statues, the best paintings of a Raphael or a Carracio. However antiquated, rough, or dismal they may appear to him at first sight, he resolves to view them over and over, till he has brought himself to relish them, and finds their hidden graces and perfections. He takes particular care to turn his eye from everything which is gaudy, luscious, and of a false taste. Nor is he less careful to turn his ear from every sort of music besides that which is of the best manner and truest harmony. . . . If a natural good taste be not already formed in us, why should not we endeavour to form it, and cultivate it till it become natural? . . .

I like! I fancy! I admire! How? By accident, or as I please? No. But I learn to fancy, to admire, to please, as the subjects themselves are deserving, and can bear me out. Otherwise, I like at this hour but dislike the next. I shall be weary of my pursuit, and, upon experience, find little pleasure in the main, if my choice and judgment in it be from no other rule than that single one, because I please. Grotesque and monstrous figures often please. Cruel spectacles and barbarities are also found to please, and, in some tempers, to please beyond all other subjects. But is this pleasure right? And shall I follow it if it presents—not strive with it, or endeavour to prevent its growth or prevalency in my temper? . . . How stands the case in a more soft and flattering kind of pleasure? . . . Effeminacy pleases me. The Indian figures, the Japan work, the enamel strikes my eye. The luscious colours and glossy paint gain

upon my fancy. A French or Flemish style is highly liked by me
at first sight, and I pursue my liking. But what ensues? . . .
Do I not for ever forfeit my good relish? How is it possible I
should thus come to taste the beauties of an Italian master, or of
a hand happily formed on nature and the ancients? 'Tis not by
wantonness and humour that I shall attain my end and arrive
at the enjoyment I propose. The art itself is severe, the rules
rigid. And if I expect the knowledge should come to me by
accident, or in play, I shall be grossly deluded, and prove
myself, at best, a mock-virtuoso or mere pedant of the kind.
          (*Treatise III: Soliloquy, or Advice to an Author*, Part III,
          Section iii.)

JOSEPH ADDISON (1672–1719): from *The Spectator*, No. 62 (1711)

Truth to Nature and Good Sense the Fundamentals in Art

   Bouhours, whom I look upon to be the most penetrating of
all the French critics, has taken pains to show, that it is impossible for any thought to be beautiful which is not just, and has
not its foundation in the nature of things; that the basis of all
wit is truth; and that no thought can be valuable, of which
good sense is not the ground-work. Boileau has endeavoured
to inculcate the same notion in several parts of his writings,
both in prose and verse. This is that natural way of writing,
that beautiful simplicity, which we so much admire in the
compositions of the ancients; and which nobody deviates from,
but those who want strength of genius to make a thought shine
in its own natural beauties. Poets who want this strength of
genius to give that majestic simplicity to nature, which we so
much admire in the works of the ancients, are forced to hunt
after foreign ornaments, and not to let any piece of wit, of
what kind soever, escape them. I look upon these writers as
Goths in poetry, who, like those in architecture, not being

able to come up to the beautiful simplicity of the old Greeks and Romans, have endeavoured to supply its place with all the extravagancies of an irregular fancy.

CHARLES GILDON (1665–1724): from *A Complete Art of Poetry* (1718)

A Rationalist Defence of the Rules

Painting is an art that requires a genius, and yet cannot be justly performed without the rules of art. The proportion of a man standing upright, is eight times the length of his head: the arms hanging straight down, reach within a span of the knee: a hand must be the length of the face, and the arms extended make the just length of the whole body. These, and an hundred more rules must be known, and followed by every painter, though of never so exalted a *genius*, or *gusto*, which can never justify him in breaking any of the rules; for those of painting, as well as those of poetry, are Nature, and show us its just lineaments, by which every judge may know the excellence or defect of the performer.

Thus in landscape the painter ought to be skilled in perspective, else can he never know the proportions, in regard of the distances, and the like. The knowing of those rules alone will not make a painter, without both a genius and practice; and in the same manner, the rules of poetry are necessary to the forming of all valuable poems, but they are not able to make a poet without genius and practice too.

In all the fine arts indeed, there has a *grotesque* and *Gothic* taste prevailed, which relishes every thing that is not natural. Thus, in general, we prefer the *Japan* pictures for the furniture of our rooms, to the fine prints of the Audrands, Simoneans, Edlinahs, and the rest of the great masters; and by the same abandoned *gusto*, we encourage operas and farces, before comedies and tragedies.

A modern wit has a very great aversion to arts and sciences, and with an air of sufficiency, avows his zeal for ignorance. But as his fancy only governs him, so are his productions most commonly sad, crude, indigested things, *like sick men's dreams*, without either head or tail. If you chance to mention art, he cries out, you are a critic, an ill-natured person; that Nature is not to be tied up to order, harmony, beauty of design; as if confusion were the only perfection.

It is, as I have observed, urged against criticism, or the rules of art, that a too regular adherence to the forms and measures of them, is a restraint on a writer's invention, and does more harm than good in composition, for that the imagination cannot so freely diffuse and expand itself, when it is obliged to any bounds or limits whatever. This argument is sometimes illustrated and supported by that famous example of an ungovernable genius in heroic virtue—I mean Alexander the Great, whose vast ambition never failed to hurry him beyond the due measures of conduct, upon which very account, say they, his exploits had always in them something wonderfully surprising and astonishing. Whereas Caesar's actions, that were more cool, deliberate, and proportioned to the rules of prudence and policy, never give us such a sublime, exalted idea of his fortitude, as we must necessarily entertain of the Greek hero's. The friends too of our great dramatic writer Shakespeare will not be persuaded, but that even his monstrous irregularities were conducive to those shining beauties which abound in most of his plays, and that if he had been more a critic, he had been less a poet; that is, if he had known more of Nature (which only the rules teach) he would have touched her less. But I say, that notwithstanding this pleasure given by Alexander's deeds, good conduct in war is no hindrance to the boldest undertakings. For any one that knows history, knows, that without it, Caesar's achievements had never been so glorious, nor most of Alexander's too. These astonishing (I might call them accidental) victories gained by the latter, betrayed (many of them at least) more of foolhardiness than valour. And a due observation of natural rules, that is, a strict attendance to the rules of Nature and Reason, can never embarrass or clog an author's fancy, but rather enlarge and extend it. They might as well urge, that good and wholesome laws that enjoin nothing but what a rational Nature would otherwise oblige us to, take away the liberty of mankind, whereas they are the very life and security of it.

For Aristotle gives not his rules as legislators do their laws, without any other reason than his will; all that he advances is confirmed by reasons drawn from the common sentiments of mankind, so that men themselves become the rule and measure of what he lays down. Thus, without considering that the rules are of almost equal date with the art they teach, or any prepossession in favour of Aristotle's name (for 'tis the work that ought to make the name valuable, and not the name the work) I find myself obliged to submit to all his decisions, the truth of which I am convinced of in myself, and whose certainty I discover by reason, and experience, which never yet deceived anybody.

To this I shall add, *The effects which these rules have produced in all ages, on different sorts of people*; and I find, that as they made the beauty of the poems of Homer, Sophocles, and Euripides in Greece, from which they were drawn, so four or five hundred years after, they adorned the poems of Virgil, and other famous Latin poets; and that now after two thousand years, they make the best tragedies we have, in which all that pleases only does so as it is conformable to these rules (and that too without one's being aware of it) and what is displeasing is such, because it is contrary to them. For good sense, and right reason, is of all countries and places; the same subjects, which caused so many tears to be shed in the Roman Theatre, produce the same effect in ours; and those things, that then gave distaste do the same now. From whence I am convinced, that never any laws had such force and authority. Human laws expire, or change very often after the death of those who enacted them, because circumstances change, and the interests of those whom they are made to serve are different; but these still gain new vigour, because they are the laws of Nature, which always acts with uniformity, renews them incessantly, and gives them a perpetuate existence.

I won't pretend, however, that the rules of this art are so firmly established, that it is impossible to add any thing to them; for though *tragedy* has all its proper parts, it is possible, that one of them may yet arrive at a greater perfection. I am persuaded, that though we have been able to add nothing to the subject, or means, yet we have added something to the manner. But all the new discoveries are so far from destroying this establishment, that they do nothing more than confirm it. For Nature is never contrary to itself.

II. THE REVIVAL OF SENTIMENT AND THE RE-EXAMINATION OF THE NATURE OF POETRY: POETRY AS THE EXPRESSION OF PASSION AND ENTHUSIASM

JOHN DENNIS (1657–1734): from *The Advancement and Reformation of Modern Poetry* (1701), Chapters V–VI

Passion is the chief thing in Poetry

As poetry is an art, it must be an imitation of Nature. That the instrument with which it makes its imitation is speech need not be disputed. That that speech must be musical no one can doubt; for numbers distinguish the parts of poetic diction from the periods of prose. Now numbers are nothing but articulate sounds, and their pauses measured by their proper proportions of time. And the periods of prosaic diction are articulate sounds, and their pauses unmeasured by such proportions. That the speech by which poetry makes its imitation must be pathetic is evident, for passion is still more necessary to it than harmony. For harmony only distinguishes its instrument from that of prose, but passion distinguishes its very nature and character. For therefore poetry is poetry, because it is more passionate and sensual than prose. A discourse that is written in very good numbers, if it wants passion, can be but measured prose. But a discourse that is everywhere extremely pathetic, and consequently everywhere bold and figurative, is certainly poetry without numbers.

Passion, then, is the characteristical mark of poetry, and consequently must be everywhere. For wherever a discourse is not pathetic there it is prosaic. As passion in a poem must be everywhere, so harmony is usually diffused throughout it. But passion answers the two ends of poetry better than harmony can do, and upon that account is preferable to it: for first it pleases more, which is evident: for passion can please without harmony, but harmony tires without passion. And in tragedy and in epic poetry a man may instruct without harmony, but never without passion: for the one instructs by admiration, and the other by compassion and terror. And as for the greater ode, if it wants passion, it becomes hateful and intolerable, and its sentences grow contemptible. . . . It is plain, then, from what has been said, that passion in poetry must be everywhere, for where there is no passion there can be no poetry, but that which we commonly call passion cannot be everywhere in any poem. There must be passion, then, that must be distinct from ordinary passion, and that must be enthusiasm. I call that ordinary passion, whose cause is clearly comprehended by him who feels it, whether it be admiration, terror, or joy; and I call the very same passions enthusiasms, when their cause is not clearly comprehended by him who feels them.

Passion is more to be derived from a Sacred Subject than from a Profane one

'Tis now our business to show that religious subjects are capable of supplying us with more frequent and stronger enthusiasms than the profane. And in order to the clearing this, let us inquire what poetical enthusiasm is. Poetical enthusiasm is a passion guided by judgment, whose cause is not comprehended by us.

Enthusiasm as well as ordinary passions must proceed from the thoughts, as the passions of all reasonable creatures must certainly do; but the reason why we know not the causes of enthusiastic as well as of ordinary passions, is because we are not so used to them, and because they proceed from thoughts, that latently and unobserved by us carry passion along with them. Here it would be no hard matter to prove that most of our thoughts are naturally attended with some sort and some degree of passion. And 'tis the expression of this passion which gives us so much pleasure, both in conversation and in human authors. For I appeal to any man who is not altogether a philosopher, whether he is not most pleased with conversation and books that are spirited. Now how can this spirit please him, but because it moves him, or what can move him but passion? We never speak for so much as a minute together without different inflexions of voice. Now any one will find upon reflection that these variations and those inflexions mark our different passions. But all this passes unregarded by us, by reason of long use, and the incredible celerity of our thoughts, whose motion is so swift that it is even to ourselves imperceptible; unless we come to reflect, and everyone will not be at the trouble of that. Now these passions, when they grow strong, I call enthusiastic motions, and the stronger they are the greater the enthusiasm must be. If any one asks what sort of passions these are, that thus unknown to us flow from these thoughts, to him I answer, that the same sort of passions flow from the thoughts that would do from the things of which those thoughts are ideas. As for example, if the thing that we think of is great, why, then admiration attends the idea of it; and if it is very great, amazement. If the thing is pleasing and delightful, why then joy and gaiety flow from the idea of it; if it is sad, melancholy; if it is mischievous and powerful, then the imagination of it is attended with terror; and if 'tis both great and likely to do hurt, and powerful, why then the thought of it is at once accompanied with wonder, terror, and astonishment. Add to all this that the mind producing these thoughts conceives by reflection a certain pride and joy and admiration, as at the conscious view of its own excellence.

Now he who strictly examines the enthusiasm that is to be met with in the greater poetry will find that it is nothing but the fore-mentioned passions, either simple or complicated, proceeding from the thoughts from which they naturally flow, as being the thoughts or images of things that carry those passions along with them.

But these passions that attend upon our thoughts are seldom so strong as they are in those kind of thoughts which we call images. For they, being the very lively pictures of the things which they represent, set them, as it were, before our very eyes. But images are never so admirably drawn as when they are drawn in motion; especially if the motion is violent. For the mind can never imagine violent motion without being in a violent agitation itself; and the imagination being fired with that agitation sets the very things before our eyes, and consequently makes us have the same passions that we should have from the things themselves. For the warmer the imagination is, the more present the things are to us of which we draw the images; and, therefore, when once the imagination is so inflamed as to get the better of the understanding, there is no difference between the images and the things themselves; as we see, for example, in fears and madmen.

Thus have we shown that enthusiasm flows from the thoughts, and consequently from the subject from which the thoughts proceed. For, as the spirit in poetry is to be proportioned to the thought—for otherwise it does not naturally flow from it, and consequently is not guided by judgment—so the thought is to be proportioned to the subject. Now no subject is so capable of supplying us with thoughts that necessarily produce these great and strong enthusiasms as a religious subject: for all which is great in religion is most exalted and amazing, all that is joyful is transporting, all that is sad is dismal, and all that is terrible is astonishing.

Isaac Watts (1674–1748): from preface to *Horæ Lyricæ* (1709)

Christian Poetry

Nor did the Blessed Spirit which animated these writers [of the Old Testament] forbid them the use of visions, dreams, the opening of scenes dreadful and delightful, and the introduction of machines upon great occasions. The divine licence in this respect is admirable and surprising, and the images are often too bold and dangerous for an uninspired writer to imitate. Mr Dennis has made a noble essay to discover how much superior is inspired poesy to the brightest and best descriptions of a mortal pen. Perhaps if his Proposal of Criticism had been encouraged and pursued, the nation might have learnt more value for the word of God, and the wits of the age might have been secured from the danger of Deism; while they must have been forced to confess at least the divinity of all the poetical books of Scripture, when they see a genius running through them more than human.

Who is there now will dare to assert that the doctrines of our holy faith will not indulge or endure a delightful dress? Shall the French poet affright us by saying

> De la foy d'un Chrêtien les Mystères terribles,
> D'Ornemens egayez ne sont point susceptibles?

But the French critic in his *Reflections upon Eloquence*, tells us "that the majesty of our religion, the holiness of its laws, the purity of its morals, the height of its mysteries, and the importance of every subject that belongs to it requires a grandeur, a nobleness, a majesty, and elevation of style suited to the theme: sparkling images and magnificent expressions must be used, and are best borrowed from Scripture: let the preacher that aims at eloquence, read the Prophets incessantly, for their writings are an abundant source of all the riches and ornaments of speech. . . ."

E

Besides, we may fetch a further answer to Mons. Boileau's objection from other poets of his own country. What a noble use have Racine and Corneille made of Christian subjects in some of their best tragedies! . . . Yet I must confess, that the *Davideis*, and the two *Arthurs*, have so far answered Boileau's objection, in English, as that the obstacles of attempting Christian poesy are broken down, and the vain pretence of its being impracticable is experimentally confuted.

With how much less toil and expense might a Dryden, an Otway, a Congreve, or a Dennis, furnish out a Christian poem, than a modern play? There is nothing amongst all the ancient Fables, or later Romances, that have two such extremes united in them, as the Eternal God becoming an Infant of Days; the Possessor of the Palace of Heaven laid to sleep in a manger; the Holy Jesus, who knew no sin, bearing the sins of men in His Body on the Tree; agonies of sorrow loading the soul of Him who was God over all, blessed for ever; and the Sovereign of Life stretching His Arms on a Cross, bleeding and expiring. The Heaven and Hell in our Divinity are infinitely more delightful and dreadful than the childish figments of a dog with three heads, the buckets of the Belides, the Furies with snaky hairs, or all the flowery stories of Elysium. And if we survey the one as themes divinely true and the other as a medley of fooleries which we can never believe, the advantage for touching the springs of passion will fall infinitely on the side of the Christian poet.

EDWARD YOUNG (1683–1765): from *On Lyric Poetry* (1728)

'Enthusiasm' in Poetry

It is the genuine character, and true merit of the ode, a little to startle some apprehensions. Men of cold complexions are very apt to mistake a want of vigour in their imaginations for a delicacy of taste in their judgments; and, like persons of a tender sight, they look on bright objects, in their natural lustre, as too glaring; what is most delightful to a stronger eye is painful to them. Thus Pindar, who has as much logic at the bottom as Aristotle or Euclid, to some critics has appeared as mad; and must appear so to all who enjoy no portion of his own divine spirit. . . .

Judgment, indeed, that masculine power of the mind, in ode, as in all compositions, should bear the supreme sway; and a beautiful imagination, as its mistress, should be subdued to its dominion. Hence, and hence only, can proceed the fairest offspring of the mind.

But then in ode, there is this difference from other kinds of poetry; that there the imagination, like a very beautiful mistress, is indulged in the appearance of domineering; though the judgment, like an artful lover, in reality carries its point; and the less it is suspected of it, it shows the more masterly conduct, and deserves the greater commendation.

It holds true in this province of writing, as in war, "The more danger, the more honour." . . . Above all, in the ode, as in every work of genius, somewhat of an original spirit should be, at least, attempted. . . . Originals only have true life, and differ as much from the best imitations, as men from the most animated pictures of them. Nor is what I say at all inconsistent with a due deference for the great standards of antiquity; nay, that very deference is an argument for it, for doubtless their example is on my side in this matter. And we should rather imitate their example in the general motives, and fundamental methods of their working, than in their works themselves. This is a distinction, I think, not hitherto made, and a distinction of consequence.

EDMUND BURKE (1729–97): from *A Philosophical Enquiry into the Origin of our Ideas of the Sublime and the Beautiful* (1756)

The Power of Words in Poetry; and the Limitations of the 'Imitation' Theory

It is one thing to make an idea clear, and another to make it affecting to the imagination. If I make a drawing of a palace, or a temple, or a landscape, I present a very clear idea of those objects; but then (allowing for the effect of imitation, which is something) my picture can at most affect only as the palace, temple, or landscape would have affected in the reality. On the other hand, the most lively and spirited verbal description I can give raises a very obscure and imperfect *idea* of such objects; but then it is in my power to raise a stronger *emotion* by the description than I could do by the best painting. This, experience constantly evinces. The proper manner of conveying the affections of the mind from one to another, is by words; there is a great insufficiency in all other methods of communication; and so far is a clearness of imagery from being absolutely necessary to an influence upon the passions, that they may be considerably operated upon, without presenting any image at all, by certain sounds adapted to that purpose; of which we have a sufficient proof in the acknowledged and powerful effects of instrumental music. In reality, a great clearness helps but little towards affecting the passions, as it is in some sort an enemy to all enthusiasms whatsoever. (Part II, Section iv.)

Poetry not strictly an Imitative Art

Hence we may observe that poetry, taken in its most general sense, cannot with strict propriety be called an art of imitation. It is indeed an imitation so far as it describes the manners and passions of men which their words can express; where *animi motus effert interprete lingua.* There it is strictly imitation; and all merely *dramatic* poetry is of this sort. But *descriptive* poetry operates chiefly by *substitution*; by means of sounds, which by custom have the effect of realities. Nothing is an imitation further than as it resembles some other thing; and words undoubtedly have no sort of resemblance to the ideas for which they stand.

Now, as words affect, not by any original power, but by representation, it might be supposed that their influence over the passions should be but light; yet it is quite otherwise; for we find by experience, that eloquence and poetry are as capable, nay indeed much more capable, of making deep and lively impressions than any other arts, and even than Nature itself in very many cases. And this arises chiefly from these three causes. First, that we take an extraordinary part in the passions of others, and that we are easily affected and brought into sympathy by any tokens which are shown of them; and there are no tokens which can express all the circumstances of most passions so fully as words; so that if a person speaks upon any subject, he can not only convey the subject to you, but likewise the manner in which he is himself affected by it. . . . Secondly, there are many things of a very affecting nature, which can seldom occur in the reality, but the words that represent them often do; and thus they have an opportunity of making a deep impression and taking root in the mind, whilst the idea of the reality was transient; and to some perhaps never really occurred in any shape, to whom it is notwithstanding very affecting, as war, death, famine, etc. Besides many ideas have never been at all presented to the senses of any men but by words, as God, angels, devils, Heaven, and Hell, all of which have, however, a great influence over the passions. Thirdly, by words we have it in our power to make such *combinations* as we cannot possibly do otherwise. By this power of combining we are able, by the addition of well-chosen circumstances, to give a new life and force to the simple object. In painting we may represent any fine figure we please; but we never can give it those enlivening touches which it may receive from words. To represent an angel in a picture, you can only draw a beautiful young man winged: but what painting can furnish out any thing so grand as the addition of one word, "the angel of the *Lord*?" It is true, I have here no clear idea; but these words affect the mind more than the sensible image did; which is all I contend for. A picture of Priam dragged to the altar's foot, and there murdered, if it were well executed, would undoubtedly be very moving; but there are very aggravating circumstances, which it could never represent:

> Sanguine fœdantem quos ipse sacraverat ignes.

As a further instance, let us consider those lines of Milton, where he describes the travels of the fallen angels through their dismal habitation:

> . . . O'er many a dark and dreary vale
> They pass'd, and many a region dolorous;
> O'er many a frozen, many a fiery Alp;
> Rocks, caves, lakes, fens, bogs, dens, and shades of death,
> A universe of death. . . .

Here is displayed the force of union in

> Rocks, caves, lakes, dens, bogs, fens, and shades,

which yet would lose the greatest part of the effect if they were not the

> Rocks, caves, lakes, dens, bogs, fens, and shades . . . of *Death*.

This idea or this affection caused by a word, which nothing but a word could annex to the others, raises a very great degree of the sublime; and this sublime is raised yet higher by what follows, a "universe of Death." Here are again two ideas not presentable but by language; and a union of them great and amazing beyond conception; if they may properly be called ideas which present no distinct image to the mind:—

but still it will be difficult to conceive how words can move the passions which belong to real objects, without representing these objects clearly. This is difficult to us, because we do not sufficiently distinguish, in our observations upon language, between a clear expression, and a strong expression. These are frequently confounded with each other, though they are in reality extremely different. The former regards the understanding; the latter belongs to the passions. The one describes a thing as it is; the latter describes it as it is felt. Now, as there is a moving tone of voice, an impassioned countenance, an agitated gesture, which affect independently of the things about which they are exerted, so there are words, and certain dispositions of words, which being peculiarly devoted to passionate subjects, and always used by those who are under the influence of any passion, touch and move us more than those which far more clearly and distinctly express the subject matter. We yield to sympathy what we refuse to description. The truth is, all verbal description, merely as naked description, though never so exact, conveys so poor and insufficient an idea of the thing described, that it could scarcely have the smallest effect if the speaker did not call in to his aid those modes of speech that mark a strong and lively feeling in himself. Then, by the contagion of our passions, we catch a fire already kindled in another, which probably might never have been struck out by the object described. (Part V, Sections vi, vii.)

III. *GENIUS AND IMAGINATION*

(*a*) THE INADEQUACY OF THE RULES: THE IDEA OF GENIUS

GEORGE FARQUHAR (1678–1707): from *Discourse upon Comedy* (1702)

The Limitations of Dramatic Criticism based on the Authority of the Rules

There are some gentlemen that have fortified their spleen so impregnably with criticism, and hold out so stiffly against all attacks of pleasantry, that the most powerful efforts of wit and humour cannot make the least impression. What a misfortune is it to these gentlemen to be natives of such an ignorant, self-willed impertinent island, where let a critic and a scholar find never so many irregularities in a play, yet five hundred saucy people will give him the lie to his face, and come to see this wicked play forty or fifty times in a year. But this *Vox Populi* is the devil, though in a place of more authority than Aristotle it is called *Vox Dei*. "Here is a play with a vengeance," (says a critic) "to bring the transaction of a year's time into the compass of three hours, to carry the whole audience with him from one kingdom to another, by the changing of a scene. Where's the probability, nay the possibility of all this? The devil's in the poet sure. He don't think to put contradictions upon us?"

Look'ee, Sir, don't be in a passion; the poet does not impose contradictions upon you, because he has told you no lie; for that only is a lie which is related with some fallacious intention that you should believe it for a truth. Now the poet expects no more that you should believe the plot of his play, than old Aesop designed the world should think his Eagle and Lion talked like you and I; which I think was every jot as improbable, as what you quarrel with; and yet the Fables took, and I'll be hanged if you yourself don't like 'em. But besides, Sir, if you are so inveterate against improbabilities, you must never come near the play-house at all; for there are several improbabilities, nay, impossibilities, that all the criticisms in Nature cannot correct; as for instance: in the part of Alexander the Great, to be affected with the transactions of the play, we must suppose that we see that great conqueror, after all his triumphs, shunned by the woman he loves, and importuned by her he hates, crossed in his cups and jollity by his own subjects, and at last miserably ending his life in a raging madness; we must suppose that we see the very Alexander, the son of Philip, in all these unhappy circumstances, else we are not touched by the moral, which represents to us the uneasiness of human life in the greatest state, and the instability of fortune in respect of worldly pomp. Yet the whole audience at the same time knows that this is Mr Betterton, who is strutting upon the stage, and tearing his lungs for a livelihood. And that the same person should be Mr Betterton and Alexander the Great at the same time, is somewhat like an impossibility, in my mind. Yet you must grant this impossibility in spite of your teeth, if you han't power to raise the old hero from the grave to act his own part.

Now for another impossibility: the less rigid critics allow to a comedy the space of an artificial day, or twenty-four hours; but those of the thorough reformation will confine it to the natural or solar day, which is but half the time. Now admitting this for a decorum absolutely requisite: this play begins when it is exactly six by your watch, and ends precisely at nine, which is the usual time of the representation. Now is it feasible, *in rerum Natura*, that the same space or extent of time can be three hours by your watch, and twelve hours upon the stage, admitting the same number of minutes, or the same measure of sand to both? I'm afraid, Sir, you must allow this for an impossiblity too; and you may with as much reason allow the play the extent of a whole year; and if you grant me a year, you may give me seven, and so to a thousand. For that a thousand years should come within the compass of three hours is no more an impossibility, than that two minutes should be contained in one. *Nullum minus continet in se majus*, is equally applicable to both.

So much for the decorum of Time; now for the regularity of Place. I might make the one a consequence of t'other, and allege that by allowing me any extent of time, you must grant me any change of place; for the one depends upon t'other; and having five or six years for the action of a play, I may travel from Constantinople to Denmark, so to France, and home to England, and rest long enough in each country besides. . . .

I am as little a friend to those rambling plays as anybody, nor have I ever espoused their party by my own practice; yet I could not forbear saying something in vindication of the great Shakespeare, whom every little fellow that can form an *Aristus primus* will presume to condemn for indecorums and absurdities—sparks that are so spruce upon their Greek and Latin, that, like our fops in travel, they can relish nothing but what is foreign, to let the world know they have been abroad forsooth.—"But it must be so, because Aristotle said it."—Now, I say it must be otherwise because Shakespeare said it, and I'm sure that Shakespeare was the greater poet of the two. But you'll say that Aristotle was the critic. . . . That's a mistake, Sir, for criticism in poetry, is no more than judgment in poetry; which you will find in your lexicon. Now if Shakespeare was the better poet, he must have the most judgment in his art; for everybody knows that judgment is an essential part of poetry, and without it no writer is worth a farthing. But to stoop to the authority of either, without consulting the reason or the consequence, is an abuse to a man's understanding; and neither the precept of the philosopher, nor example of the poet, should go down with me, without examining the weight of their assertions. We can expect no more decorum or regularity in any business, than the nature of the thing will bear. Now, if the stage cannot subsist without the strength of supposition and force of fancy in the audience; why should a poet fetter the business of his plot, and starve his action, for the nicety of an hour, or the change of a scene; since the thought of man can fly over a thousand years with the same ease, and in the same instant of time, that your eye glances from the figure of six to seven on the dial-plate; and can glide from the Cape of Good-Hope to the Bay of St Nicholas, which is quite across the world, with the same quickness and activity, as between Covent-Garden Church, and Will's Coffee-House. Then I must beg of these gentlemen to let our old English authors alone. . . . If they have left vice unpunished, virtue unrewarded, folly unexposed, or prudence unsuccessful, the contrary of which is the *utile* of comedy, let them be lashed to some purpose. If any part of their plots have been independent of the rest, or any of their characters forced or unnatural— which destroys the *dulce* of plays—let them be hissed off the stage. But if, by a true decorum in these material points, they have writ successfully, and answered the end of dramatic poetry in every respect, let them rest in peace, and their memories enjoy the encomiums due to their merit, without any reflection for waiving those niceties, which are neither instructive to the world, nor diverting to mankind, but are like all the rest of critical learning, fit only to set people together by the ears in ridiculous controversies, that are not one jot material to the good of the public, whether they be true or false.

JOSEPH ADDISON (1672–1719): from *The Spectator*, Nos. 160,
592 (1711–12)

The Definition of Genius: Genius and the Rules

There is no character more frequently given to a writer, than
that of being a genius. I have heard many a little sonneteer
called a fine genius. There is not an heroic scribbler in the
nation, that has not his admirers, who think him a great
genius; and as for your smatterers in tragedy, there is scarce a
man among them who is not cried up by one or other for a
prodigious genius.

My design in this paper is to consider what is properly a
great genius, and to throw some thoughts together on so
uncommon a subject.

Among great geniuses, those few draw the admiration of all
the world upon them, and stand up as the prodigies of mankind,
who by the mere strength of natural parts, and without any
assistance of art or learning, have produced works that were
the delight of their own times, and the wonder of posterity.
There appears something nobly wild and extravagant in these
great natural geniuses, that is infinitely more beautiful than
all the turn and polishing of what the French call a *Bel Esprit*,
by which they would express a genius refined by conversation,
reflection, and the reading of the most polite authors. The
greatest genius which runs through the arts and sciences, takes
a kind of tincture from them, and falls unavoidably into
imitation.

Many of these great natural geniuses, that were never
disciplined and broken by rules of art, are to be found among
the ancients, and, in particular, among those of the more
eastern parts of the world. Homer has innumerable flights
that Virgil was not able to reach; and in the Old Testament we
find several passages more elevated and sublime than any in

Homer. At the same time that we allow a greater and more daring genius to the ancients, we must own that the greatest of them very much failed in, or, if you will, that they were much above, the nicety and correctness of the moderns. In their similitudes and allusions, provided there was a likeness, they did not much trouble themselves about the decency of the comparison: thus Solomon resembles the nose of his beloved to the tower of Lebanon which looketh toward Damascus, as the coming of a thief in the night is a similitude of the same kind in the New Testament. It would be endless to make collections of this nature: Homer illustrates one of his heroes encompassed with the enemy, by an ass in a field of corn, that has his sides belaboured by all the boys of the village without stirring a foot for it; and another of them tossing to and fro in his bed, and burning with resentment, to a piece of flesh broiled on the coals. This particular failure in the ancients opens a large field of raillery to the little wits, who can laugh at an indecency, but not relish the sublime in these sorts of writings. The present emperor of Persia, conformable to this eastern way of thinking, amidst a great many pompous titles, denominates himself the Sun of Glory, and the Nutmeg of Delight. In short, to cut off all cavilling against the ancients, and particularly those of the warmer climates, who had most heat and life in their imaginations, we are to consider that the rule of observing what the French call the *Bienséance* in an allusion has been found out of latter years, and in the colder regions of the world; where we would make some amends for our want of force and spirit, by a scrupulous nicety and exactness in our compositions. Our countryman Shakespeare was a remarkable instance of this first kind of great geniuses. . . .

There is another kind of great geniuses which I shall place in a second class, not as I think them inferior to the first, but only for distinction's sake, as they are of a different kind. This second class of great geniuses are those that have formed themselves by rules, and submitted the greatness of their natural talents to the corrections and restraints of art. Such among the Greeks were Plato and Aristotle; among the Romans, Virgil and Tully; among the English, Milton and Sir Francis Bacon.

The genius in both these classes of authors may be equally great, but shows itself after a different manner. In the first it is like a rich soil in a happy climate, that produces a whole wilderness of noble plants, rising in a thousand beautiful landscapes, without any certain order or regularity. In the other it is the same rich soil under the same happy climate, that has been laid out in walks and parterres, and cut into shape and beauty by the skill of the gardener.

The great danger in these latter kind of geniuses is, lest they cramp their own abilities too much by imitation, and form themselves altogether upon models, without giving the full play to their own natural parts. An imitation of the best authors is not to compare with a good original; and I believe we may observe that very few writers make an extraordinary figure in the world, who have not something in their way of thinking or expressing themselves, that is peculiar to them, and entirely their own. . . . (No. 160.)

I have a great esteem for a true critic, such as Aristotle and Longinus among the Greeks, Horace and Quintilian among the Romans, Boileau and Dacier among the French. But it is our misfortune, that some who set up for professed critics among us are so stupid, that they do not know how to put ten words together with elegance or common propriety, and withal so illiterate, that they have no taste of the learned languages, and therefore criticise upon old authors only at second-hand. They judge of them by what others have written, and not by any notions thay have of the authors themselves. The words unity, action, sentiment, and diction, pronounced with an air of authority, give them a figure among unlearned readers, who are apt to believe they are very deep, because they are unintelli-

gible. The ancient critics are full of the praises of their contemporaries; they discover beauties which escaped the
observation of the vulgar, and very often find out reasons for
palliating and excusing such little slips and oversights as were
committed in the writings of eminent authors. On the contrary, most of the smatterers in criticism who appear among us
make it their business to vilify and depreciate every new
production that gains applause, to descry imaginary blemishes,
and to prove, by far-fetched arguments, that what pass for
beauties in any celebrated piece, are faults and errors. In
short, the writings of these critics compared with those of the
ancients, are like the works of the sophists compared with
those of the old philosophers.

Envy and cavil are the natural fruits of laziness and
ignorance; which was probably the reason, that in the heathen
mythology Momus is said to be the son of Nox and Somnus,
of Darkness and Sleep. Idle men, who have not been at the
pains to accomplish or distinguish themselves, are very apt to
detract from others; as ignorant men are very subject to
decry those beauties in a celebrated work which they have not
eyes to discover. Many of our sons of Momus, who dignify
themselves by the name of critics, are the genuine descendants
of these two illustrious ancestors. They are often led into
those numerous absurdities, in which they daily instruct the
people, by not considering that, first, There is sometimes a
greater judgment shown in deviating from the rules of art,
than in adhering to them; and, secondly, That there is more
beauty in the works of a great genius who is ignorant of all the
rules of art, than in the works of a little genius, who not only
knows, but scrupulously observes them.

First, we may often take notice of men who are perfectly
acquainted with all the rules of good writing, and notwithstanding choose to depart from them on extraordinary
occasions. I could give instances out of all the tragic writers of
antiquity who have shown their judgment in this particular,

and purposely receded from an established rule of the drama, when it has made way for a much higher beauty than the observation of such a rule would have been. Those who have surveyed the noblest pieces of architecture and statuary, both ancient and modern, know very well that there are frequent deviations from art in the works of the greatest masters, which have produced a much nobler effect than a more accurate and exact way of proceeding could have done. This often arises from what the Italians call the *gusto grande* in these arts, which is what we call the sublime in writing.

In the next place, our critics do not seem sensible that there is more beauty in the works of a great genius who is ignorant of the rules of art, than in those of a little genius who knows and observes them. It is of these men of genius that Terence speaks, in opposition to the little artificial cavillers of his time:

> Quorum æmulari exoptat negligentiam
> Potius, quam istorum obscuram diligentiam.

A critic may have the same consolation in the ill success of his play, as Dr South tells us a physician has at the death of a patient—that he was killed *secundum artem*. Our inimitable Shakespeare is a stumbling-block to the whole tribe of these rigid critics. Who would not rather read one of his plays, where there is not a single rule of the stage observed, than any production of a modern critic, where there is not one of them violated? Shakespeare was indeed born with all the seeds of poetry, and may be compared to the stone in Pyrrhus's ring, which, as Pliny tells us, had the figure of Apollo and the nine Muses in the veins of it, produced by the spontaneous hand of nature, without any help from art. (No. 592.)

SAMUEL JOHNSON (1709–84): from *The Rambler*, Nos. 125 and
156 (1751), and the preface to Shakespeare (1765)

The Rules discussed in Relation to Shakespeare: the Powers
of Genius illustrated from his Plays

Definitions have been no less difficult or uncertain in
criticisms than in law. Imagination, a licentious and vagrant
faculty, unsusceptible of limitations, and impatient of restraint,
has always endeavoured to baffle the logician, to perplex the
confines of distinction, and burst the enclosures of regularity.
There is, therefore, scarcely any species of writing, of which we
can tell what is its essence, and what are its constituents; every
new genius produces some innovation, which, when invented
and approved, subverts the rules which the practice of foregoing authors had established. (*The Rambler*, No. 125.)

It ought to be the first endeavour of a writer to distinguish
Nature from custom; or that which is established because it is
right, from that which is right only because it is established;
that he may neither violate essential principles by a desire of
novelty, nor debar himself from the attainment of beauties
within his view, by a needless fear of breaking rules which no
literary dictator had authority to enact. (*The Rambler*, No. 156.)

Shakespeare's Plays the Work of a Rich, Inventive Genius

His plots, whether historical or fabulous, are always crowded
with incidents, by which the attention of a rude people was
more easily caught than by sentiment or argumentation; and
such is the power of the marvellous, even over those who
despise it, that every man finds his mind more strongly seized
by the tragedies of Shakespeare than of any other writer;
others please us by particular speeches, but he always makes us

F

anxious for the event, and has perhaps excelled all but Homer in securing the first purpose of a writer, by exciting restless and unquenchable curiosity, and compelling him that reads his work to read it through.

The shows and bustle with which his plays abound have the same original. As knowledge advances, pleasure passes from the eye to the ear, but returns, as it declines, from the ear to the eye. Those to whom our author's labours were exhibited had more skill in pomps or processions than in poetical language, and perhaps wanted some visible and discriminated events, as comments on the dialogue. He knew how he should most please; and whether his practice is more agreeable to Nature, or whether his example has prejudiced the nation, we still find that on our stage something must be done as well as said, and inactive declamation is very coldly heard, however musical or elegant, passionate or sublime.

Voltaire expresses his wonder, that our author's extravagancies are endured by a nation which has seen the tragedy of *Cato*. Let him be answered, that Addison speaks the language of poets, and Shakespeare, of men. We find in *Cato* innumerable beauties which enamour us of its author, but we see nothing that acquaints us with human sentiments or human actions; we place it with the fairest and the noblest progeny which judgment propagates by conjunction with learning; but *Othello* is the vigorous and vivacious offspring of observation impregnated by genius. *Cato* affords a splendid exhibition of artificial and fictitious manners, and delivers just and noble sentiments, in diction easy, elevated, and harmonious, but its hopes and fears communicate no vibration to the heart; the composition refers us only to the writer; we pronounce the name of *Cato*, but we think on *Addison*.

The work of a correct and regular writer is a garden accurately formed and diligently planted, varied with shades and scented with flowers; the composition of Shakespeare is a forest, in which oaks extend their branches, and pines tower in the air, interspersed sometimes with weeds and brambles, and sometimes giving shelter to myrtles and to roses; filling the eye with awful pomp, and gratifying the mind with endless diversity. Other poets display cabinets of precious rarities, minutely finished, wrought into shape, and polished into brightness. Shakespeare opens a mine which contains gold and diamonds in unexhaustible plenty, though clouded by incrustations, debased by impurities, and mingled with a mass of meaner minerals.

Shakespeare's use of Tragi-comedy a Source of Imaginative Truth

The censure which he has incurred by mixing comic and tragic scenes, as it extends to all his works, deserves more consideration. Let the fact be first stated, and then examined.

Shakespeare's plays are not in the rigorous and critical sense either tragedies or comedies, but compositions of a distinct kind; exhibiting the real state of sublunary Nature, which partakes of good and evil, joy and sorrow, mingled with endless variety of proportion and innumerable modes of combination; and expressing the course of the world, in which the loss of one is the gain of another; in which, at the same time, the reveller is hasting to his wine, and the mourner burying his friend; in which the malignity of one is sometimes defeated by the frolic of another; and many mischiefs and many benefits are done and hindered without design. . . .

Shakespeare has united the powers of exciting laughter and sorrow not only in one mind, but in one composition. Almost all his plays are divided between serious and ludicrous characters, and, in the successive evolutions of the design, sometimes produce seriousness and sorrow, and sometimes levity and laughter.

That this is a practice contrary to the rules of criticism will be readily allowed; but there is always an appeal open from criticism to Nature. The end of writing is to instruct; the end of poetry is to instruct by pleasing. That the mingled drama may convey all the instruction of tragedy or comedy cannot be denied, because it includes both in its alternations of exhibition, and approaches nearer than either to the appearance of life, by showing how great machinations and slender designs may promote or obviate one another, and the high and the low co-operate in the general system by unavoidable concatenation.

Shakespeare's Disregard of the Unities of Place and Time a Mark of Genius. The True Nature of Dramatic Representation

It will be thought strange, that, in enumerating the defects of this writer, I have not yet mentioned his neglect of the unities, his violation of those laws which have been instituted and established by the joint authority of poets and of critics.

For his other deviations from the art of writing, I resign him to critical justice, without making any other demand in his favour, than that which must be indulged to all human excellence; that his virtues be rated with his failings: but, from the censure which this irregularity may bring upon him, I shall, with due reverence to that learning which I must oppose, adventure to try how I can defend him.

His histories, being neither tragedies nor comedies, are not subject to any of their laws; nothing more is necessary to all the praise which they expect, than that the changes of action be so prepared as to be understood, that the incidents be various and affecting, and the characters consistent, natural, and distinct. No other unity is intended, and therefore none is to be sought.

In his other works he has well enough preserved the unity of action. He has not, indeed, an intrigue regularly perplexed and regularly unravelled; he does not endeavour to hide his design only to discover it, for this is seldom the order of real events, and Shakespeare is the poet of Nature: but his plan has commonly what Aristotle requires, a beginning, a middle, and an end; one event is concatenated with another, and the conclusion follows by easy consequence. There are perhaps some incidents that might be spared, as in other poets there is much talk that only fills up time upon the stage; but the general system makes gradual advances, and the end of the play is the end of expectation.

To the unities of time and place he has shown no regard; and perhaps a nearer view of the principles on which they stand will diminish their value, and withdraw from them the veneration which, from the time of Corneille, they have very generally received, by discovering that they have given more trouble to the poet, than pleasure to the auditor.

The necessity of observing the unities of time and place arises from the supposed necessity of making the drama credible. The critics hold it impossible that an action of months or years can be possibly believed to pass in three hours; or that the spectator can suppose himself to sit in the theatre, while ambassadors go and return between distant kings, while armies are levied and towns besieged, while an exile wanders and returns, or till he whom they saw courting his mistress, shall lament the untimely fall of his son. The mind revolts from evident falsehood, and fiction loses its force when it departs from the resemblance of reality. From the narrow limitation of time necessarily arises the contraction of place. The spectator, who knows that he saw the first act at Alexandria, cannot suppose that he sees the next at Rome, at a distance to which not the dragons of Medea could, in so short a time, have transported him; he knows with certainty that he has not changed his place; and he knows that place cannot change itself; that what was a house cannot become a plain; that what was Thebes can never be Persepolis.

Such is the triumphant language with which a critic exults over the misery of an irregular poet, and exults commonly without resistance or reply. It is time therefore to tell him, by

the authority of Shakespeare, that he assumes, as an unquestion-
able principle, a position, which, while his breath is forming it
into words, his understanding pronounces to be false. It is
false that any representation is mistaken for reality; that any
dramatic fable in its materiality was ever credible, or, for a
single moment, was ever credited.

The objection arising from the impossibility of passing
the first hour at Alexandria, and the next at Rome, supposes
that when the play opens the spectator really imagines himself
at Alexandria, and believes that his walk to the theatre has been
a voyage to Egypt, and that he lives in the days of Antony and
Cleopatra. Surely he that imagines this may imagine more.
He that can take the stage at one time for the palace of the
Ptolemies, may take it in half an hour for the promontory of
Actium. Delusion, if delusion be admitted, has no certain
limitation; if the spectator can be once persuaded that his
old acquaintance are Alexander and Cæsar, that a room
illuminated with candles is the plain of Pharsalia, or the bank
of Granicus, he is in a state of elevation above the reach of
reason, or of truth, and from the heights of empyrean poetry
may despise the circumscriptions of terrestrial nature. There is
no reason why a mind thus wandering in ecstasy should count
the clock, or why an hour should not be a century in that
calenture of the brains that can make the stage a field.

The truth is that the spectators are always in their senses,
and know, from the first act to the last, that the stage is only
the stage, and that the players are only players. They come to
hear a certain number of lines recited with just gesture and
elegant modulation. The lines relate to some action, and an
action must be in some place; but the different actions that
complete a story may be in places very remote from each other;
and where is the absurdity of allowing that space to represent
first Athens, and then Sicily, which was always known to be
neither Sicily nor Athens, but a modern theatre.

By supposition, as place is introduced, time may be extended;

the time required by the fable elapses for the most part between the acts; for, of so much of the action as is represented, the real and poetical duration is the same. If, in the first act, preparations for war against Mithridates are represented to be made in Rome, the event of the war may, without absurdity, be represented, in the catastrophe, as happening in Pontus; we know that there is neither war, nor preparation for war; we know that we are neither in Rome nor Pontus; that neither Mithridates nor Lucullus are before us. The drama exhibits successive imitations of successive actions, and why may not the second imitation represent an action that happened years after the first; if it be so connected with it, that nothing but time can be supposed to intervene. Time is, of all modes of existence, most obsequious to the imagination; a lapse of years is as easily conceived as a passage of hours. In contemplation we easily contract the time of real actions, and therefore willingly permit it to be contracted when we only see their imitation.

It will be asked how the drama moves, if it is not credited. It is credited with all the credit due to a drama. It is credited, whenever it moves, as a just picture of a real original; as representing to the auditor what he would himself feel, if he were to do or suffer what is there feigned to be suffered or to be done. The reflection that strikes the heart is not that the evils before us are real evils, but that they are evils to which we ourselves may be exposed. If there be any fallacy, it is not that we fancy the players, but that we fancy ourselves unhappy for a moment; but we rather lament the possibility than suppose the presence of misery, as a mother weeps over her babe, when she remembers that death may take it from her. The delight of tragedy proceeds from our consciousness of fiction; if we thought murders and treasons real, they would please no more.

Imitations produce pain or pleasure, not because they are mistaken for realities, but because they bring realities to

mind. When the imagination is recreated by a painted landscape, the trees are not supposed capable to give us shade, or
the fountains coolness; but we consider how we should be
pleased with such fountains playing beside us, and such woods
waving over us. We are agitated in reading the history of
Henry the Fifth, yet no man takes his book for the field of
Agincourt. A dramatic exhibition is a book recited with
concomitants that increase or diminish its effect. Familiar
comedy is often more powerful on the theatre, than in the
page; imperial tragedy is always less. The humour of Petruchio
may be heightened by grimace; but what voice or what
gesture can hope to add dignity or force to the soliloquy of
Cato?

A play read affects the mind like a play acted. It is therefore
evident that the action is not supposed to be real; and it follows
that between the acts a longer or shorter time may be allowed
to pass, and that no more account of space or duration is to be
taken by the auditor of a drama, than by the reader of a narra-
tive, before whom may pass in an hour the life of a hero, or the
revolutions of an empire.

Whether Shakespeare knew the unities, and rejected them
by design, or deviated from them by happy ignorance, it is,
I think, impossible to decide, and useless to enquire. We may
reasonably suppose that, when he rose to notice, he did not
want the counsels and admonitions of scholars and critics,
and that he at last deliberately persisted in a practice which he
might have begun by chance. As nothing is essential to the
fable but unity of action, and as the unities of time and place
arise evidently from false assumptions, and, by circumscribing
the extent of the drama, lessen its variety, I cannot think it
much to be lamented that they were not known by him, or not
observed: nor, if such another poet could arise, should I very
vehemently reproach him, that his first act passed at Venice,
and his next in Cyprus. Such violations of rules merely
positive become the comprehensive genius of Shakespeare, and

such censures are suitable to the minute and slender criticism of Voltaire:

> Non usque adeo permiscuit imis
> Longus summa dies, ut non, si voce Metelli
> Serventur leges, malint a Cæsare tolli.

Yet when I speak thus slightly of dramatic rules, I cannot but recollect how much wit and learning may be produced against me; before such authorities I am afraid to stand, not that I think the present question one of those that are to be decided by mere authority, but because it is to be suspected that these precepts have not been so easily received but for better reasons than I have yet been able to find. The result of my enquiries, in which it would be ludicrous to boast of impartiality, is that the unities of time and place are not essential to a just drama, that though they may sometimes conduce to pleasure, they are always to be sacrificed to the nobler beauties of variety and instruction; and that a play written with nice observation of critical rules, is to be contemplated as an elaborate curiosity, as the product of superfluous and ostentatious art, by which is shown rather what is possible than what is necessary.

He that, without diminution of any other excellence, shall preserve all the unities unbroken, deserves the like applause with the architect who shall display all the orders of architecture in a citadel, without any deduction from its strength; but the principal beauty of a citadel is to exclude the enemy; and the greatest graces of a play are to copy nature, and instruct life.

Perhaps what I have here not dogmatically but deliberately written, may recall the principles of the drama to a new examination. I am almost frighted at my own temerity; and when I estimate the fame and the strength of those that maintain the contrary opinion, am ready to sink down in reverential silence; as Æneas withdrew from the defence of Troy, when he saw Neptune shaking the wall, and Juno heading the besiegers. (*Preface to Shakespeare*.)

EDWARD YOUNG (1683–1765): from *Conjectures on Original Composition in a Letter to the Author of "Sir Charles Grandison"* (1759)

Genius and Imitation: the True Relationship between the Moderns and the Ancients

The mind of a man of genius is a fertile and pleasant field, pleasant as Elysium, and fertile as Tempe; it enjoys a perpetual spring. Of that spring, originals are the fairest flowers; imitations are of quicker growth, but fainter bloom. Imitations are of two kinds; one of Nature, one of authors. The first we call *originals*, and confine the term *imitation* to the second. I shall not enter into the curious enquiry of what is, or is not, strictly speaking, original, content with what all must allow, that some compositions are more so than others; and the more they are so, I say, the better. Originals are, and ought to be, great favourites, for they are great benefactors; they extend the republic of letters, and add a new province to its dominion; imitators only give us a sort of duplicate of what we had, possibly much better, before; increasing the mere drug of books, while all that makes them valuable—knowledge and genius—are at a stand. The pen of an original writer, like Armida's wand, out of a barren waste calls a blooming spring: Out of that blooming spring an imitator is a transplanter of laurels, which sometimes die on removal, always languish in a foreign soil.

But suppose an imitator to be most excellent (and such there are), yet still he but nobly builds on another's foundation; his debt is, at least, equal to his glory; which therefore, on the balance, cannot be very great. On the contrary, an original, though but indifferent (its originality being set aside), yet has something to boast; it is something to say with him in Horace, *Meo sum Pauper in aere*, and to share ambition with no less than

Cæsar, who declared he had rather be the first in a village than the second at Rome.

Still farther: an imitator shares his crown, if he has one, with the chosen object of his imitation; an original enjoys an undivided applause. An original may be said to be of a vegetable nature; it rises spontaneously from the vital root of genius; it grows, it is not made. Imitations are often a sort of manufacture wrought up by those mechanics, art and labour, out of pre-existent materials not their own. . . .

But why are originals so few? Not because the writer's harvest is over, the great reapers of antiquity having left nothing to be gleaned after them; nor because the human mind's teeming time is past, or because it is incapable of putting forth unprecedented births; but because illustrious examples engross, prejudice, and intimidate. They engross our attention, and so prevent a due inspection of ourselves; they prejudice our judgment in favour of their abilities, and so lessen the sense of our own; and they intimidate us with the splendour of their renown, and thus under diffidence bury our strength. Nature's impossibilities, and those of diffidence lie wide asunder.

Let it not be suspected that I would weakly insinuate any thing in favour of the moderns, as compared with ancient authors; no, I am lamenting their great inferiority. But I think it is no *necessary* inferiority; that it is not from divine destination, but from some cause far beneath the moon: I think that human souls, through all periods, are equal; that due care and exertion would set us nearer our immortal predecessors than we are at present; and he who questions and confutes this, will show abilities not a little tending toward a proof of that equality which he denies.

After all, the first ancients had no merit in being originals: they could not be imitators. Modern writers have a choice to make; and therefore have a merit in their power. They may soar in the regions of liberty, or move in the soft fetters of easy imitation; and imitation has as many plausible reasons to urge, as Pleasure had to offer to Hercules. Hercules made the choice of an hero, and so became immortal.

Yet let not assertors of classic excellence imagine that I deny the tribute it so well deserves. He that admires not ancient authors, betrays a secret he would conceal, and tells the world that he does not understand them. Let us be as far from neglecting, as from copying, their admirable compositions: sacred be their rights, and inviolable their fame. Let our understanding feed on theirs; they afford the noblest nourishment; but let them nourish, not annihilate, our own. When we read, let our imagination kindle at their charms; when we write, let our judgment shut them out of our thoughts; treat even Homer himself as his royal admirer was treated by the cynic; bid him stand aside, nor shade our composition from the beams of our own genius; for nothing original can rise, nothing immortal can ripen, in any other sun.

Must we then, you say, not imitate ancient authors? Imitate them, by all means; but imitate aright. He that imitates the divine *Iliad*, does not imitate Homer; but he who takes the same method, which Homer took, for arriving at a capacity of accomplishing a work so great. Tread in his steps to the sole fountain of immortality; drink where he drank, at the true Helicon, that is, at the breast of Nature. Imitate; but imitate not the *composition*, but the *man*. For may not this paradox pass into a maxim? *viz.*, "The less we copy the renowned ancients, we shall resemble them the more." . . .

What glory to come near, what glory to reach, what glory (presumptuous thought!) to surpass, our predecessors! And is that then in Nature absolutely impossible? Or is it not, rather, contrary to Nature to fail in it? Nature herself sets the ladder; all wanting is our ambition to climb. For by the bounty of Nature we are as strong as our predecessors; and by the favour of time (which is but another round in Nature's scale) we stand on higher ground. As to the first, were they more than men? Or are we less? Are not our minds cast in the same mould with those before the flood? The flood affected matter; mind escaped. As to the second; though we are moderns, the world is an ancient; more ancient far, than when they, whom we most admire, filled it with their fame. Have we not their beauties, as stars, to guide; their defects, as rocks, to be shunned; the judgment of ages on both, as a chart to conduct, and a sure helm to steer us in our passage to greater perfection than theirs? And shall we be stopped in our rival pretensions to fame by this just reproof?

Stat contra, dicitque tibi tua pagina, fur es.

MARTIAL

It is by a sort of noble contagion, from a general familiarity with their writings, and not by any particular sordid theft, that we can be the better for those who went before us. Hope we, from plagiarism, any dominion in literature; as that of Rome arose from a nest of thieves?

Rome was a powerful ally to many states; ancient authors are our powerful allies; but we must take heed, that they do not succour, till they enslave, after the manner of Rome. Too formidable an idea of their superiority, like a spectre, would fright us out of a proper use of our wits; and dwarf our understanding, by making a giant of theirs. Too great awe for them lays genius under restraint, and denies it that free scope, that full elbow-room, which is requisite for striking its most masterly strokes. Genius is a master-workman; learning is but an instrument; and an instrument, though most valuable, yet not always indispensable. Heaven will not admit of a partner in the accomplishment of some favourite spirits; but rejecting all human means, assumes the whole glory to itself. Have not some, though not famed for erudition, so written, as almost to persuade us, that they shone brighter, and soared higher, for escaping the boasted aid of that proud ally?

Nor is it strange; for what, for the most part, mean we by

genius, but the power of accomplishing great things without the means generally reputed necessary to that end? A genius differs from a good understanding as a magician from a good architect: that raises his structure by means invisible; this by the skilful use of common tools. Hence genius has ever been supposed to partake of something divine. *Nemo unquam vir magnus fuit, sine aliquo afflatu divino.*

Learning, destitute of this superior aid, is fond, and proud, of what has cost it much pains; is a great lover of rules, and boaster of famed examples: as beauties less perfect, who owe half their charms to cautious art, learning inveighs against natural unstudied graces, and small harmless inaccuracies, and sets rigid bounds to that liberty, to which genius often owes its supreme glory; but the no-genius its frequent ruin. For unprescribed beauties, and unexampled excellence, which are characteristics of genius, lie without the pale of learning's authorites and laws; which pale, genius must leap to come at them. But by that leap, if genius is wanting, we break our necks; we lose that little credit, which possibly we might have enjoyed before. For rules, like crutches, are a needful aid to the lame, though an impediment to the strong. A Homer casts them away; and, like his Achilles,

Jura negat sibi nata, nihil non arrogat,

by native force of mind. There is something in poetry beyond prose-reason; there are mysteries in it not to be explained, but admired; which render mere prose-men infidels to their divinity. . . .

Moreover, so boundless are the bold excursions of the human mind, that, in the vast void beyond real existence, it can call forth shadowy beings, and unknown worlds, as numerous, as bright, and, perhaps, as lasting, as the stars; such quite-original beauties we may call paradisaical.

Natos sine semine flores.
Ovid

When such an ample area for renowned adventure in original attempts lies before us, shall we be as mere leaden pipes, conveying to the present age small streams of excellence from its grand reservoir in antiquity; and those too, perhaps, muddied in the pass? Originals shine, like comets; have no peer in their path; are rivalled by none, and the gaze of all. All other compositions (if they shine at all) shine in clusters; like the stars in the galaxy; where, like bad neighbours, all suffer from all; each particular being diminished, and almost lost in the throng.

If thoughts of this nature prevailed; if ancients and moderns were no longer considered as masters and pupils, but as hard-matched rivals for renown; then moderns, by the longevity of their labours, might, one day, become ancients themselves. And old Time, that best weigher of merits, to keep his balance even, might have the golden weight of an *Augustan* age in both his scales: or rather our scale might descend; and that of antiquity (as a modern match for it strongly speaks) might *kick the beam*.

And why not? For, consider, since an impartial Providence scatters talents indifferently, as through all orders of persons, so through all periods of time; since a marvellous light, unenjoyed of old, is poured on us by revelation, with larger prospects extending our understanding, with brighter objects enriching our imagination, with an inestimable prize setting our passions on fire, thus strengthening every power that enables composition to shine; since there has been no fall in man on this side Adam, who left no works, and the works of all other ancients are our auxiliars against themselves, as being perpetual spurs to our ambition, and shining lamps in our path to fame; since this World is a school, as well for intellectual, as moral, advance; and the longer human nature is at school, the better scholar it should be; since as the moral World expects its glorious millennium, the World intellectual may hope, by the rules of analogy, for some superior degrees of excellence to crown her later scenes; nor may it only hope, but must enjoy them too; for Tully, Quintilian, and all true critics allow, that virtue assists genius, and that the writer will be more able, when better is the man—all these particulars, I say, considered, why should it seem altogether impossible, that Heaven's latest editions of the human mind may be the most correct, and fair; that the day may come, when the moderns may proudly look back on the comparative darkness of former ages, on the children of antiquity; reputing Homer and Demosthenes as the dawn of divine genius; and Athens as the cradle of infant fame? What a glorious revolution would this make in the rolls of renown!

(*b*) THE THEORY OF IMAGINATION

JOSEPH ADDISON (1672–1719): from *The Spectator*, Nos. 411–412, 416, 418–420 (1712)

The Nature of Imagination and its Dependence on the Sense of Sight

Our sight is the most perfect and most delightful of all our senses. It fills the mind with the largest variety of ideas, converses with its objects at the greatest distance, and continues the longest in action without being tired or satiated with its proper enjoyments. The sense of feeling can indeed give us a notion of extension, shape, and all other ideas that enter at the eye, except colours; but at the same time it is very much straitened and confined in its operations, to the number, bulk and distance of its particular objects. Our sight seems designed to supply all these defects, and may be considered as a more delicate and diffusive kind of touch, that spreads itself over an infinite multitude of bodies, comprehends the largest figures, and brings into our reach some of the most remote parts of the universe.

It is this sense which furnishes the imagination with its ideas; so that by the pleasures of the imagination or fancy (which I shall use promiscuously) I here mean such as arise from visible objects, either when we have them actually in our view, or when we call up their ideas into our minds by paintings, statues, descriptions, or any the like occasion. We cannot indeed have a single image in the fancy that did not make its first entrance through the sight: but we have the power of retaining, altering and compounding those images, which we have once received, into all the varieties of picture and vision that are most agreeable to the imagination; for by this faculty a man in a dungeon is capable of entertaining himself with scenes and landscapes more beautiful than any that can be found in the whole compass of Nature.

There are few words in the English language which are employed in a more loose and uncircumscribed sense than those of the fancy and the imagination. I therefore thought it necessary to fix and determine the notion of these two words, as I intend to make use of them in the thread of my following speculations, that the reader may conceive rightly what is the subject which I proceed upon. I must therefore desire him to remember, that by the pleasures of the imagination, I mean only such pleasures as arise originally from sight, and that I divide these pleasures into two kinds: my design being first of all to discourse of those primary pleasures of the imagination, which entirely proceed from such objects as are before our eyes; and in the next place to speak of those secondary pleasures of the imagination which flow from the ideas of visible objects, when the objects are not actually before the eye, but are called up into our memories, or formed into agreeable visions of things that are either absent or fictitious.

The pleasures of the imagination, taken in the full extent, are not so gross as those of sense, nor so refined as those of the understanding. The last are, indeed, more preferable, because they are founded on some new knowledge or improvement in

G

the mind of man; yet it must be confessed that those of the imagination are as great and as transporting as the other. A beautiful prospect delights the soul, as much as a demonstration; and a description in Homer has charmed more readers than a chapter in Aristotle. Besides, the pleasures of the imagination have this advantage, above those of the understanding, that they are more obvious, and more easy to be acquired. It is but opening the eye, and the scene enters. The colours paint themselves on the fancy, with very little attention of thought or application of mind in the beholder. We are struck, we know not how, with the symmetry of anything we see, and immediately assent to the beauty of an object, without enquiring into the particular causes and occasions of it. (No. 411.)

I shall first consider those pleasures of the imagination which arise from the actual view and survey of outward objects; and these, I think, all proceed from the sight of what is *great*, *uncommon*, or *beautiful*. There may, indeed, be something so terrible or offensive, that the horror or loathsomeness of an object may over-bear the pleasure which results from its *greatness*, *novelty* or *beauty*; but still there will be such a mixture of delight in the very disgust it gives us, as any of these three qualifications are most conspicuous and prevailing.

By *greatness*, I do not only mean the bulk of any single object, but the largeness of a whole view, considered as one entire piece. Such are the prospects of an open champain country, a vast uncultivated desert, of huge heaps of mountains, high rocks and precipices, or a wide expanse of waters, where we are not struck with the novelty or beauty of the sight, but with that rude kind of magnificence which appears in many of these stupendous works of Nature. Our imagination loves to be filled with an object, or to grasp at any thing that is too big for its capacity. We are flung into a pleasing astonishment at such unbounded views, and feel a delightful stillness and amazement in the soul at the apprehension of them. The mind of man naturally hates everything that looks like a restraint upon it, and is apt to fancy itself under a sort of confinement, when the sight is pent up in a narrow compass, and shortened on every side by the neighbourhood of walls or mountains. On the contrary, a spacious horizon is an image of liberty, where the eye has room to range abroad, to expatiate at large on the immensity of its views, and to lose itself amidst the variety of objects that offer themselves to its observation. Such wide and undetermined prospects are as pleasing to the fancy, as the speculations of eternity or infinitude are to the understanding. But if there be a beauty or uncommonness joined with this grandeur, as in a troubled ocean, a heaven adorned with stars and meteors, or a spacious landscape cut out into rivers, woods, rocks, and meadows, the pleasure still grows upon us, as it arises from more than a single principle.

Everything that is *new* or *uncommon* raises a pleasure in the imagination, because it fills the soul with an agreeable surprise, gratifies its curiosity, and gives it an idea of which it was not before possessed. We are indeed so often conversant with one set of objects, and tired out with so many repeated shows of the same things, that whatever is *new* or *uncommon* contributes a little to vary human life, and to divert our minds, for a while, with the strangeness of its appearance: it serves us for a kind of refreshment, and takes off from that satiety we are apt to complain of in our usual and ordinary entertainments. It is this that bestows charms on a monster, and makes even the imperfections of Nature please us. It is this that recommends variety, where the mind is every instant called off to something new, and the attention not suffered to dwell too long and waste itself on any particular object. It is this, likewise, that improves what is great or beautiful, and makes it afford the mind a double entertainment. Groves, fields, and meadows, are at any season of the year pleasant to look upon, but never so much as in the opening of the spring, when they are all new and fresh, with their first gloss upon them, and not yet too much accustomed and familiar to the eye. For this reason there is nothing that more enlivens a prospect than rivers, jetteaus, or falls of water, where the scene is perpetually shifting, and entertaining the sight every moment with something that is new. We are quickly tired with looking upon hills and valleys, where everything continues fixed and settled in the same place and posture, but find our thoughts a little agitated and relieved at the sight of such objects as are ever in motion, and sliding away from beneath the eye of the beholder.

But there is nothing that makes its way more directly to the soul than *beauty*, which immediately diffuses a secret satisfaction and complacency through the imagination, and gives a finishing to anything that is great or uncommon. The very first discovery of it strikes the mind with an inward joy, and spreads a cheerfulness and delight through all its faculties. There is not perhaps any real beauty or deformity more in one piece of matter than another, because we might have been so made, that whatsoever now appears loathsome to us, might have shown itself agreeable; but we find by experience, that there are several modifications of matter which the mind, without any previous consideration, pronounces at first sight beautiful or deformed. Thus we see that every different species of sensible creatures has its different notions of beauty, and that each of them is most affected with the beauties of its own kind. This is nowhere more remarkable than in birds of the same shape and proportion, where we often see the male determined in his courtship by the single grain or tincture of a feather, and never discovering any charms but in the colour of its species. . . .

There is a second kind of beauty that we find in the several products of Art and Nature, which does not work in the imagination with that warmth and violence as the beauty that appears in our proper species, but is apt however to raise in us a secret delight, and a kind of fondness for the places or objects in which we discover it. This consists either in the gaiety or variety of colours, in the symmetry and proportion of parts, in the arrangement and disposition of bodies, or in a just mixture and concurrence of all together. Among these several kinds of beauty the eye takes most delight in colours. We nowhere meet with a more glorious or pleasing show in Nature, than what appears in the heavens at the rising and setting of the sun, which is wholly made up of those different stains of light that show themselves in clouds of a different situation. For this reason we find the poets, who are always addressing themselves to the imagination, borrowing more of their epithets from colours than from any other topic.

As the fancy delights in everything that is great, strange, or beautiful, and is still more pleased the more it finds of these perfections in the same object, so it is capable of receiving a new satisfaction by the assistance of another sense. Thus any continued sound, as the music of birds, or a fall of water, awakens every moment the mind of the beholder, and makes him more attentive to the several beauties of the place that lie before him. Thus, if there arises a fragrancy of smells or perfumes, they heighten the pleasures of the imagination, and make even the colours and verdure of the landscape appear more agreeable; for the ideas of both senses recommend each other, and are pleasanter together, than when they enter the mind separately; as the different colours of a picture, when they are well disposed, set off one another, and receive an additional beauty from the advantage of their situation. (No. 412.)

The 'Secondary Pleasures' of Imagination

I at first divided the pleasures of the imagination, into such as arise from objects that are actually before our eyes, or that once entered in at our eyes, and are afterwards called up into the mind either barely by its own operations, or on occasion of something without us, as statues, or descriptions. We have already considered the first division, and shall therefore enter on the other, which, for distinction's sake, I have called the secondary pleasures of the imagination. When I say the ideas we receive from statues, descriptions, or such like occasions, are the same that were once actually in our view, it must not be understood that we had once seen the very place, action, or person which are carved or described. It is sufficient that we have seen places, persons, or actions in general, which bear a resemblance, or at least some remote analogy with what we find represented, since it is in the power of the imagination, when it is once stocked with particular ideas, to enlarge, compound, and vary them at her own pleasure. . . .

In all these instances, this secondary pleasure of the imagination proceeds from that action of the mind, which compares the ideas arising from the original objects, with the ideas we receive from the statue, picture, description, or sound that represents them. It is impossible for us to give the necessary reason, why this operation of the mind is attended with so much pleasure, as I have before observed on the same occasion; but we find a great variety of entertainments derived from this single principle. For it is this that not only gives us a relish of statuary, painting, and description, but makes us delight in all the actions and arts of mimicry. It is this that makes the several kinds of wit pleasant, which consists, as I have formerly shown, in the affinity of ideas. And we may add, it is this also that raises the little satisfaction we sometimes find in the different sorts of false wit; whether it consist in the affinity of letters, as an anagram, acrostic; or of syllables, as in doggerel rimes, echoes; or of words, as in puns, quibbles; or of a whole sentence or poem, to wings, and altars. The *final cause*, probably, of annexing pleasure to this operation of the mind, was to quicken and encourage us in our searches after truth, since the distinguishing one thing from another, and the right discerning betwixt our ideas, depends wholly upon our comparing them together, and observing the congruity or disagreement that appears among the several works of Nature.

But I shall here confine myself to those pleasures of the imagination which proceed from ideas raised by *words*, because most of the observations that agree with descriptions, are equally applicable to painting and statuary.

Words, when well chosen, have so great a force in them, that a description often gives us more lively ideas than the sight of things themselves. The reader finds a scene drawn in stronger colours, and painted more to the life in his imagination, by the help of words, than by an actual survey of the scene which they describe. In this case the poet seems to get the better of Nature; he takes, indeed, the landscape after her, but gives it more vigorous touches, heightens its beauty, and so enlivens the whole piece, that the images which flow from the objects themselves appear weak and faint in comparison of those that come from the expressions. The reason, probably, may be because in the survey of any object, we have only so much of it painted on the imagination as comes in at the eye; but in its description, the poet gives us as free a view of it as he pleases, and discovers to us several parts, that either we did not attend to, or that lay out of our sight when we first beheld it. As we look on any object, our idea of it is, perhaps, made up of two or three simple ideas; but when the poet represents it, he may either give us a more complex idea of it, or only raise in us such ideas as are most apt to affect the imagination. (No. 416.)

Our Pleasure in the Artistic Representation of what is in itself Disagreeable. The Idealizing Power of Imagination

The pleasures of these secondary views of the imagination, are of a wider and more universal nature than those it has when joined with sight; for not only what is great, strange or beautiful, but anything that is disagreeable when looked upon, pleases us in an apt description. Here, therefore, we must

enquire after a new principle of pleasure, which is nothing else
but the action of the mind, which *compares* the ideas that
arise from words, with the ideas that arise from the objects
themselves; and why this operation of the mind is attended
with so much pleasure, we have before considered. For this
reason therefore, the description of a dunghill is pleasing to
the imagination, if the image be represented to our minds by
suitable expressions; though, perhaps, this may be more
properly called the pleasure of the understanding than of the
fancy, because we are not so much delighted with the image
that is contained in the description, as with the aptness of the
description to excite the image.

But if the description of what is little, common or deformed,
be acceptable to the imagination, the description of what is
great, surprising or beautiful, is much more so; because here
we are not only delighted with *comparing* the representation
with the original, but are highly pleased with the original
itself. Most readers, I believe, are more charmed with Milton's
description of Paradise, than of Hell; they are both, perhaps,
equally perfect in their kind, but in the one the brimstone and
sulphur are not so refreshing to the imagination, as the beds
of flowers and the wilderness of sweets in the other.

There is yet another circumstance which recommends a
description more than all the rest, and that is, if it represents to
us such objects as are apt to raise a secret ferment in the mind of
the reader, and to work with violence upon his passions. For,
in this case, we are at once warmed and enlightened, so that
the pleasure becomes more universal, and is several ways
qualified to entertain us. Thus, in painting, it is pleasant to
look on the picture of any face, where the resemblance is hit,
but the pleasure increases, if it be the picture of a face that is
beautiful, and is still greater, if the beauty be softened with an
air of melancholy or sorrow. The two leading passions which
the more serious parts of poetry endeavour to stir up in us, are
terror and pity. And here, by the way, one would wonder how

it comes to pass, that such passions as are very unpleasant at all other times, are very agreeable when excited by proper descriptions. It is not strange, that we should take delight in such passages as are apt to produce hope, joy, admiration, love, or the like emotions in us, because they never rise in the mind without an inward pleasure which attends them. But how comes it to pass, that we should take delight in being terrified or dejected by a description, when we find so much uneasiness in the fear or grief which we receive from any other occasion?

If we consider, therefore, the nature of this pleasure, we shall find that it does not arise so properly from the description of what is terrible, as from the reflection we make on ourselves at the time of reading it. When we look on such hideous objects, we are not a little pleased to think we are in no danger of them. We consider them at the same time as dreadful and harmless; so that the more frightful appearance they make, the greater is the pleasure we receive from the sense of our own safety. In short, we look upon the terrors of a description with the same curiosity and satisfaction that we survey a dead monster.

> Informe cadaver
> Protrahitur: nequeunt expleri corda tuendo
> Terribiles oculos, vultum, villosaque setis
> Pectora semiferi, atque extinctos faucibus ignes.
> VIRGIL

It is for the same reason that we are delighted with the reflecting upon dangers that are past, or in looking on a precipice at a distance, which would fill us with a different kind of horror, if we saw it hanging over our heads.

In the like manner, when we read of torments, wounds, deaths, and the like dismal accidents, our pleasure does not flow so properly from the grief which such melancholy descriptions give us, as from the secret comparison which we make between ourselves and the person who suffers. Such representations teach us to set a just value upon our own condition, and make us prize our good fortune, which exempts us from the like calamities. This is, however, such a kind of pleasure as we are not capable of receiving, when we see a person actually lying under the tortures that we meet with in a description; because, in this case, the object presses too close upon our senses, and bears so hard upon us, that it does not give us time or leisure to reflect on ourselves. Our thoughts are so intent upon the miseries of the sufferer, that we cannot turn them upon our own happiness. Whereas, on the contrary, we consider the misfortunes we read in history or poetry, either as past or as fictitious, so that the reflection upon ourselves rises in us insensibly, and over-bears the sorrow we conceive for the sufferings of the afflicted.

But because the mind of man requires something more perfect in matter than what it finds there, and can never meet with any sight in Nature which sufficiently answers its highest ideas of pleasantness; or, in other words, because the imagination can fancy to itself things more great, strange, or beautiful than the eye ever saw, and is still sensible of some defect in what it has seen; on this account it is the part of a poet to humour the imagination in its own notions, by mending and perfecting Nature where he describes a reality, and by adding greater beauties than are put together in Nature, where he describes a fiction.

He is not obliged to attend her in the slow advances which she makes from one season to another, or to observe her conduct in the successive production of plants and flowers. He may draw into his description all the beauties of the spring and autumn, and make the whole year contribute something to render it the more agreeable. . . . In a word, he has the modelling of Nature in his own hands, and may give her what charms he pleases, provided he does not reform her too much, and run into absurdities by endeavouring to excel. (No. 418.)

*The 'Fairy Way of Writing': the Charm of Fantasy
or Inventive Imagination*

There is a kind of writing wherein the poet quite loses sight of Nature, and entertains his reader's imagination with the characters and actions of such persons as have many of them no existence but what he bestows on them. Such are fairies, witches, magicians, demons, and departed spirits. This Mr Dryden calls *the fairy way of writing*, which is, indeed, more difficult than any other that depends on the poet's fancy, because he has no pattern to follow in it, and must work altogether out of his own invention.

There is a very odd turn of thought required for this sort of writing, and it is impossible for a poet to succeed in it, who has not a particular cast of fancy, and an imagination naturally fruitful and superstitious. Besides this, he ought to be very well versed in legends and fables, antiquated romances, and the traditions of nurses and old women, that he may fall in with our natural prejudices, and humour those notions which we have imbibed in our infancy. For, otherwise, he will be apt to make his fairies talk like people of his own species, and not like other sets of beings, who converse with different objects, and think in a different manner from that of mankind;

> Sylvis deducti caveant, me judice, Fauni
> Ne velut innati triviis, ac pene forenses,
> Aut nimium teneris juvenentur versibus . . .
>
> HORACE

I do not say with Mr Bayes in the *Rehearsal*, that spirits must not be confined to speak sense, but it is certain their sense ought to be a little discoloured, that it may seem particular, and proper to the person and condition of the speaker.

These descriptions raise a pleasing kind of horror in the mind of the reader, and amuse his imagination with the strangeness and novelty of the persons who are represented in them. They bring up into our memory the stories we have heard in our childhood, and favour those secret terrors and apprehensions to which the mind of man is naturally subject. We are pleased with surveying the different habits and behaviours of foreign countries; how much more must we be delighted and surprised when we are led, as it were, into a new creation, and see the persons and manners of another species? Men of cold fancies and philosophical dispositions object to this kind of poetry, that it has not probability enough to affect the imagination. But to this it may be answered, that we are sure, in general, there are many intellectual beings in the World besides ourselves, and several species of spirits, who are subject to different laws and economies from those of mankind; when we see, therefore, any of these represented naturally, we cannot look upon the representation as altogether impossible; nay, many are prepossessed with such false opinions, as dispose them to believe these particular delusions; at least, we have all heard so many pleasing relations in favour of them, that we do not care for seeing through the falsehood, and willingly give ourselves up to so agreeable an imposture.

The Ancients have not much of this poetry among them, for, indeed, almost the whole substance of it owes its original to the darkness and superstition of later ages, when pious frauds were made use of to amuse mankind, and frighten them into a sense of their duty. Our forefathers looked upon Nature with more reverence and horror, before the world was enlightened by learning and philosophy, and loved to astonish themselves with the apprehensions of witchcraft, prodigies, charms and enchantments. There was not a village in England that had not a ghost in it, the church-yards were all haunted, every large common had a circle of fairies belonging to it, and there was scarce a shepherd to be met with who had not seen a spirit.

Among all the poets of this kind our English are much the

best, by what I have yet seen, whether it be that we abound with more stories of this nature, or that the genius of our country is fitter for this sort of poetry. For the English are naturally fanciful, and very often disposed by that gloominess and melancholy of temper, which is so frequent in our nation, to many wild notions and visions, to which others are not so liable.

Among the English, Shakespeare has incomparably excelled all others. That noble extravagance of fancy, which he had in so great perfection, thoroughly qualified him to touch this weak, superstitious part of his reader's imagination; and made him capable of succeeding, where he had nothing to support him besides the strength of his own genius. There is something so wild and yet so solemn in the speeches of his ghosts, fairies, witches and the like imaginary persons, that we cannot forbear thinking them natural, though we have no rule by which to judge of them, and must confess, if there are such beings in the world, it looks highly probable they should talk and act as he has represented them.

There is another sort of imaginary beings, that we some-times meet with among the poets, when the author represents any passion, appetite, virtue or vice, under a visible shape, and makes it a person or an actor in his poem. Of this nature are the descriptions of Hunger and Envy in Ovid, of Fame in Virgil, and of Sin and Death in Milton. We find a whole creation of the like shadowy persons in Spenser, who had an admirable talent in representations of this kind. . . . Thus we see how many ways poetry addresses itself to the imagina-tion, as it has not only the whole circle of Nature for its province, but makes new worlds of its own, shows us persons who are not to be found in being, and represents even the faculties of the soul, with her several virtues and vices, in a sensible shape and character. (No. 419.)

The Function of Imagination in History and in Science:
the Imagination and the Understanding compared

As the writers in poetry and fiction borrow their several
materials from outward objects, and join them together at their
own pleasure, there are others who are obliged to follow Nature
more closely, and to take entire scenes out of her. Such are
historians, natural philosophers, travellers, geographers, and
in a word, all who describe visible objects of a real existence.

It is the most agreeable talent of an historian to be able to
draw up his armies and fight his battles in proper expressions,
to set before our eyes the divisions, cabals and jealousies of
great men, and to lead us step by step into the several actions
and events of his history. We love to see the subject unfolding
itself by just degrees, and breaking upon us insensibly, that so
we may be kept in a pleasing suspense, and have time given us
to raise our expectations, and to side with one of the parties
concerned in the relation. I confess this shows more the art
than the veracity of the historian, but I am only to speak of
him as he is qualified to please the imagination. And in this
respect Livy has, perhaps, excelled all who went before him,
or have written since his time. He describes everything
in so lively a manner, that his whole *History* is an admirable
picture, and touches on such proper circumstances in every
story, that his reader becomes a kind of spectator, and feels in
himself all the variety of passions which are correspondent to
the several parts of the relation.

But among this set of writers, there are none who more
gratify and enlarge the imagination, than the authors of the
new philosophy, whether we consider their theories of the
Earth or Heavens, the discoveries they have made by glasses,
or any other of their contemplations on Nature. We are not
a little pleased to find every green leaf swarm with millions of
animals, that at their largest growth are not visible to the

naked eye. There is something very engaging to the fancy, as well as to our reason, in the treatises of metals, minerals, plants, and meteors. But when we survey the whole Earth at once, and the several planets that lie within its neighbourhood, we are filled with a pleasing astonishment, to see so many worlds hanging one above another, and sliding round their axles in such an amazing pomp and solemnity. If, after this, we contemplate those wide fields of Ether, that reach in height as far as from Saturn to the fixed stars, and run abroad almost to an infinitude, our imagination finds its capacity filled with so immense a prospect, and puts itself upon the stretch to comprehend it. But if we may yet rise higher, and consider the fixed stars as so many vast oceans of flame, that are each of them attended with a different set of planets, and still discover new firmaments and new lights, that are sunk farther in those unfathomable depths of Ether, so as not to be seen by the strongest of our telescopes, we are lost in such a labyrinth of suns and worlds, and confounded with the immensity and magnificence of Nature. . . .

I have dwelt the longer on this subject, because I think it may show us the proper limits, as well as the defectiveness, of our imagination; how it is confined to a very small quantity of space, and immediately stopped in its operations, when it endeavours to take in anything that is very great or very little. Let a man try to conceive the different bulk of an animal, which is twenty, from another which is a hundred times less than a mite, or to compare in his thoughts a length of a thousand diameters of the Earth with that of a million, and he will quickly find that he has no different measures in his mind, adjusted to such extraordinary degrees of grandeur or minuteness. The understanding, indeed, opens an infinite space on every side of us, but the imagination, after a few faint efforts, is immediately at a stand, and finds herself swallowed up in the immensity of the void that surrounds it. Our reason can pursue a particle of matter through an infinite variety of divisions, but the fancy soon loses sight of it, and feels in itself a kind of chasm, that wants to be filled with matter of a more sensible bulk. We can neither widen nor contract the faculty to the dimensions of either extreme. The object is too big for our capacity, when we would comprehend the circumference of a world, and dwindles into nothing when we endeavour after the idea of an atom.

It is possible this defect of imagination may not be in the soul itself, but as it acts in conjunction with the body. Perhaps there may not be room in the brain for such a variety of impressions, or the animal spirits may be incapable of figuring them in such a manner, as is necessary to excite so very large or very minute ideas. However it be, we may well suppose that beings of a higher nature very much excel us in this respect, as it is probable the soul of Man will be infinitely more perfect hereafter in this faculty, as well as in all the rest; insomuch that, perhaps, the imagination will be able to keep pace with the understanding, and to form in itself distinct ideas of all the different modes and quantities of space. (No. 420.)

JOSEPH WARTON (1722–1800): from the Dedication to *An Essay on the Genius and Writings of Pope* (1756)

Imagination the Soul of Poetry

We do not, it should seem, sufficiently attend to the difference there is between a Man of Wit, a Man of Sense, and a true Poet. Donne and Swift were undoubtedly men of wit, and men of sense: but what traces have they of pure poetry? It is remarkable that Dryden says of Donne: "He was the greatest wit, though not the greatest poet, of this nation." Fontenelle and La Motte are entitled to the former character; but what can they urge to gain the latter? Which of these characters is the most valuable and useful, is entirely out of the question: all

I plead for, is to have their several provinces kept distinct from each other; and to impress on the reader, that a clear head and acute understanding are not sufficient alone to make a poet; that the most solid observations on human life, expressed with the utmost elegance and brevity, are *morality* and not *poetry*; that the *Epistles* of Boileau in rhyme are no more poetical than the *Characters* of La Bruyère in prose; and that it is a creative and glowing *imagination, acer spiritus ac vis,* and that alone, that can stamp a writer with this exalted and very uncommon character, which so few possess, and of which so few can properly judge.

For one person who can adequately relish, and enjoy a work of imagination, twenty are to be found who can taste and judge of observations on familiar life and the manners of the age. . . .

The sublime and the pathetic are the two chief nerves of all genuine poesy. What is there transcendently sublime or pathetic in Pope?

RICHARD HURD (1720–1808): from *Letters on Chivalry and Romance, X* (1762)

The Nature of Imaginative Truth

The only criticism, indeed, that is worth regarding is the philosophical. But there is a sort which looks like philosophy, and is not. May not that be the case here?

This criticism, whatever name it deserves, supposes that the poets, who are liars by profession, expect to have their lies believed. Surely they are not so unreasonable. They think it enough, if they can but bring you to *imagine* the possibility of them.

And how small a matter will serve for this? A legend, a tale, a tradition, a rumour, a superstition; in short, any

H

thing is enough to be the basis of their air-formed visions. Does any capable reader trouble himself about the truth, or even the credibility, of their fancies? Alas, no; he is best pleased when he is made to conceive (he minds not by what magic) the existence of such things as his reason tells him did not, and were never likely to, exist. . . .

So little account does this wicked poetry make of philosophical or historical truth: all she allows us to look for, is *poetical truth*; a very slender thing indeed, and which the poet's eye, when rolling in its finest frenzy, can but just lay hold of. To speak in the philosophic language of Mr Hobbes, it is something much *beyond the actual bounds, and only within the conceived possibility, of nature.*

But the source of bad criticism, as universally of bad philosophy, is the abuse of terms. A poet, they say, must 'follow Nature'; and by Nature we are to suppose can only be meant the known and experienced course of affairs in this World. Whereas the poet has a world of his own, where experience has less to do than consistent imagination.

He has, besides, a supernatural world to range in. He has Gods, and Faeries, and Witches at his command: and,

> O! who can tell
> The hidden pow'r of herbes, and might of magic spell?
> SPENSER. B.i. C.2.

Thus in the poet's world all is marvellous and extraordinary; yet not unnatural in one sense, as it agrees to the conceptions that are readily entertained of these magical and wonder-working Natures.

This trite maxim of 'following Nature' is further mistaken in applying it indiscriminately to all sorts of poetry.

In those species which have men and manners professedly for their theme, a strict conformity with human nature is reasonably demanded.

> Non hic Centauros, non Gorgonas, Harpyiasque
> Invenies: hominem pagina nostra sapit:

is a proper motto to a book of epigrams, but would make a poor figure at the head of an epic poem.

Still further, in those species that address themselves to the heart and would obtain their end, not through the imagination, but through the passions, there the liberty of transgressing Nature, I mean the real powers and properties of human nature, is infinitely restrained; and *poetical* truth is, under these circumstances, almost as severe a thing as *historical*.

The reason is, we must first believe, before we can be affected.

But the case is different with the more sublime and creative poetry. This species, addressing itself solely or principally to the imagination (a young and credulous faculty, which loves to admire and to be deceived) has no need to observe those cautious rules of credibility so necessary to be followed by him who would touch the affections and interest the heart.

This difference, you will say, is obvious enough. How came it then to be overlooked? From another mistake, in extending a particular precept of the drama into a general maxim.

The *incredulus odi* of Horace ran in the heads of these critics, though his own words confine the observation singly to the stage.

> Segnius irritant animos demissa per aurem
> Quam quae sunt oculis subjecta fidelibus, et quae
> Ipse sibi tradit Spectator . . .

That which passes in *representation* and challenges, as it were, the scrutiny of the eye, must be truth itself, or something very nearly approaching to it. But what passes in *narration*, even on the stage, is admitted without much difficulty:

> . . . multaque tolles
> Ex oculis, quae mox narret facundia praesens.

In the epic narration, which may be called *absens facundia*, the reason of the thing shows this indulgence to be still greater. It appeals neither to the eye nor the ear, but simply to the imagination, and so allows the poet a liberty of multi-plying and enlarging his impostures at pleasure, in proportion to the easiness and comprehension of that faculty.

These general reflexions hardly require an application to the present subject. The tales of faery are exploded as fantastic and incredible. They would merit this contempt, if presented on the stage; I mean, if they were given as the proper subject of dramatic imitation, and the interest of the poet's plot were to be wrought out of the adventures of these marvellous persons. But the epic muse runs no risk in giving way to such fanciful exhibitions.

You may call them, as one does, "extraordinary dreams, such as excellent poets and painters, by being over studious, may have in the beginning of fevers."

The epic poet would acknowledge the charge, and even value himself upon it. He would say, "I leave to the sage dramatist the merit of being always broad awake, and always in his senses: the *divine dream*, and delirious fancy, are among the noblest of my prerogatives." . . .

Thus you see the apology of the Italian poets is easily made on every supposition. But I stick to my point and maintain that the fairy tales of Tasso do him more honour than what are called the more natural, that is, the classical parts of his poem. His imitations of the ancients have indeed their merit; for he was a genius in everything. But they are faint and cold and almost insipid, when compared with his original fictions. We make a shift to run over the passages he has copied from Virgil. We are all on fire amidst the magical feats of Ismen, and the enchantments of Armida.

> Magnanima mensogna, hor quando è il vero
> Si bello, che si possa à te preporre?

I speak at least for myself; and must freely own, if it were not for these *lies* of Gothic invention, I should scarcely be disposed to give the *Gierusalemme Liberata* a second reading. . . .

The pagan Gods, and Gothic Fairies were equally out of credit, when Milton wrote. He did well therefore to supply their room with angels and devils. If these too should wear out of the popular creed (and they seem in a hopeful way, from the liberty some late critics have taken with them) I know not what other expedients the epic poet might have recourse to; but this I know, the pomp of verse, the energy of description, and even the finest moral paintings would stand him in no stead. Without *admiration* (which cannot be effected but by the marvellous of celestial intervention—I mean, the agency of superior natures really existing, or by the illusion of the fancy taken to be so) no epic poem can be long-lived.

I am not afraid to instance in the *Henriade* itself; which, notwithstanding the elegance of the composition, will in a short time be no more read than the *Gondibert* of Sir W. Davenant, and for the same reason.

Critics may talk what they will of *Truth and Nature*, and abuse the Italian poets, as they will, for transgressing both in their incredible fictions. But believe it, my friend, these fictions with which they have studied to delude the world, are of that kind of creditable deceits, of which a wise ancient pronounces with assurance, *That they, who deceive, are honester than they who do not deceive; and they, who are deceived, wiser than they who are not deceived.*

IV. *THE IDEA OF TASTE AND THE PERSISTENCE OF CLASSICAL DOCTRINE*

EDMUND BURKE (1729–97): from *On Taste* (1759)

Taste, Sensibility, and Judgment

I mean by the word 'Taste' no more than that faculty or those faculties of the mind, which are affected with, or which form a judgment of, the works of imagination and the elegant arts. This is, I think, the most general idea of that word, and what is the least connected with any particular theory. And my point in this enquiry is, to find whether there are any principles, on which the imagination is affected, so common to all, so grounded and certain, as to supply the means of reasoning satisfactorily about them. And such principles of taste I fancy there are; however paradoxical they may seem to those, who on a superficial view imagine that there is so great a diversity of tastes, both in kind and degree, that nothing can be more indeterminate.

All the natural powers in man, which I know, that are conversant about external objects, are the senses, the imagination, and the judgment. And first with regard to the senses. We do and we must suppose, that as the conformation of their organs are nearly or altogether the same in all men, so the manner of perceiving external objects is in all men the same, or with little difference. We are satisfied that what appears to be light to one eye, appears light to another; that what seems sweet to one palate, is sweet to another; that what is dark and bitter to this man, is likewise dark and bitter to that; and we conclude in the same manner of great and little, hard and soft, hot and cold, rough and smooth; and indeed of all the natural qualities and affections of bodies. If we suffer ourselves to imagine that their senses present to different men different images of things, this sceptical proceeding will make every sort of reasoning on every subject vain and frivolous, even that sceptical reasoning itself which had persuaded us to entertain a doubt concerning the agreement of our perceptions. But as there will be little doubt that bodies present similar images to the whole species, it must necessarily be allowed, that the pleasures and the pains which every object excites in one man, it must raise in all mankind, whilst it operates naturally, simply, and by its proper powers only. . . .

Besides the ideas, with their annexed pains and pleasures, which are presented by the sense, the mind of man possesses a sort of creative power of its own, either in representing at pleasure the images of things in the order and manner in which they were received by the senses, or in combining those images in a new manner, and according to a different order. This power is called imagination; and to this belongs whatever is called wit, fancy, invention, and the like. But it must be observed, that this power of the imagination is incapable of producing any thing absolutely new; it can only vary the disposition of those ideas which it has received from the senses. Now the imagination is the most extensive province of pleasure and pain, as it is the region of our fears and our hopes, and of all our passions that are connected with them; and whatever is calculated to affect the imagination with these commanding ideas, by force of any original natural impression, must have the same power pretty equally over all men. For since the imagination is only the representation of the senses, it can only be pleased or displeased with the images, from the same principle on which the sense is pleased or displeased with the realities; and consequently there must be just as close an agreement in the imaginations as in the senses of men. A little attention will convince us that this must of necessity be the case.

. . . . .

So long as we are conversant with the sensible qualities of things, hardly any more than the imagination seems concerned; little more also than the imagination seems concerned when the passions are represented, because by the force of natural sympathy they are felt in all men without any recourse to reasoning, and their justness recognised in every mind; and they do not affect it in an arbitrary or casual manner, but upon certain, natural, and uniform principles. But as many of the works of imagination are not confined to the representation of sensible objects, nor to efforts upon the passions, but extend themselves to the manners, the characters, the actions, and designs of men, their relations, their virtues and vices, they come within the province of the judgment, which is improved by attention, and by the habit of reasoning. All these make a very considerable part of what are considered as the objects of taste; and Horace sends us to the schools of philosophy and the world for our instruction in them. Whatever certainty is to be acquired in morality and the science of life, just the same degree of certainty have we in what relates to them in works of imitation. Indeed it is for the most part in our skill in manners, and in the observances of time and place, and of decency in general, which is only to be learned in those schools to which Horace recommends us, that what is called taste, by way of distinction, consists; and which is in reality no other than a more refined judgment. On the whole, it appears to me, that what is called taste, in its most general acceptation, is not a simple idea, but is partly made up of a perception of the primary pleasures of sense, of the secondary pleasures of the imagination, and of the conclusions of the reasoning faculty, concerning the various relations of these, and concerning the human passions, manners, and actions. All this is requisite to form taste, and the ground-work of all these is the same in the human mind; for as the senses are the great originals of all our ideas, and consequently of all our pleasures, if they are not uncertain and arbitrary, the whole ground-work of taste is common to all, and therefore there is a sufficient foundation for a conclusive reasoning on these matters.

Whilst we consider taste merely according to its nature and species, we shall find its principles entirely uniform; but the degree in which these principles prevail, in the several individuals of mankind, is altogether as different as the principles themselves are similar. For sensibility and judgment, which are the qualities that compose what we commonly call a *taste*, vary exceedingly in various people. From a defect in the former of these qualities arises a want of taste; a weakness in the latter constitutes a wrong or a bad one. There are some men formed with feelings so blunt, with tempers so cold and phlegmatic, that they can hardly be said to be awake during the whole course of their lives. Upon such persons the most striking objects make but a faint and obscure impression. There are others so continually in the agitation of gross and merely sensual pleasures, or so occupied in the low drudgery of avarice, or so heated in the chase of honours and distinction, that their minds, which had been used continually to the storms of these violent and tempestuous passions, can hardly be put in motion by the delicate and refined play of the imagination. These men, though from a different cause, become as stupid and insensible as the former; but whenever either of these happen to be struck with any natural elegance or greatness, or with these qualities in any work of art, they are moved upon the same principle.

The cause of a wrong taste is a defect of judgment. And this may arise from a natural weakness of understanding (in whatever the strength of that faculty may consist), or, which is much more commonly the case, it may arise from a want of a proper and well-directed exercise, which alone can make it strong and ready. Besides that ignorance, inattention, prejudice, rashness, levity, obstinacy, in short, all those passions, and all those vices, which pervert the judgment in other matters, prejudice it no less in this its more refined and elegant province. These causes produce different opinions upon every thing which is an object of the understanding, without inducing us to suppose that there are no settled principles of reason. And indeed on the whole one may observe, that there is rather less difference upon matters of taste among mankind, than upon most of those which depend upon the naked reason; and that men are far better agreed on the excellence of a description in Virgil, than on the truth or falsehood of a theory of Aristotle.

A rectitude of judgment in the arts, which may be called a good taste, does in a great measure depend upon sensibility; because if the mind has no bent to the pleasures of the imagination, it will never apply itself sufficiently to works of that species to acquire a competent knowledge in them. But, though a degree of sensibility is requisite to form a good judgment, yet a good judgment does not necessarily arise from a quick sensibility of pleasure; it frequently happens that a very poor judge, merely by force of a greater complexional sensibility, is more affected by a very poor piece, than the best judge by the most perfect; for as everything new, extraordinary, grand, or passionate, is well calculated to affect such a person, and as the faults do not affect him, his pleasure is more pure and unmixed; and as it is merely a pleasure of the imagination, it is much higher than any which is derived from a rectitude of the judgment; the judgment is for the greater part employed in throwing stumbling-blocks in the way of the imagination, in dissipating the scenes of its enchantment, and in tying us down to the disagreeable yoke of our reason: for almost the only pleasure that men have in judging better than others, consists in a sort of conscious pride and superiority, which arises from thinking rightly; but then, this is an indirect pleasure, a pleasure which does not immediately result from the object which is under contemplation. In the morning of our days, when the senses are unworn and tender, when the whole man is awake in every part, and the gloss of novelty fresh upon all the objects that surround us, how lively at that time are our sensations, but how false and inaccurate the judgments we form of things! I despair of ever receiving the same degree of pleasure from the most excellent performances of genius, which I felt at that age from pieces which my present judgment regards as trifling and contemptible.

.   .   .   .   .

Before I leave this subject, I cannot help taking notice of an opinion which many persons entertain, as if the taste were a separate faculty of the mind, and distinct from the judgment and imagination; a species of instinct, by which we are struck naturally, and at the first glance, without any previous reasoning, with the excellencies, or the defects, of a composition. So far as the imagination and the passions are concerned, I believe it true that the reason is little consulted; but where disposition, where decorum, where congruity are concerned, in short wherever the best taste differs from the worst, I am convinced that the understanding operates, and nothing else; and its operation is in reality far from being always sudden, or, when it is sudden, it is often far from being right. Men of the best taste, by consideration come frequently to change these early and precipitate judgments, which the mind, from its aversion to neutrality and doubt, loves to form on the spot. It is known that the taste (whatever it is) is improved exactly as we improve our judgment, by extending our knowledge, by a steady attention to our object, and by frequent exercise. They who have not taken these methods, if their taste decides quickly, it is always uncertainly; and their quickness is owing to their presumption and rashness, and not to any sudden irradiation, that in a moment dispels all darkness from their minds. But they who have cultivated that species of knowledge which makes the object of taste, by degrees, and habitually, attain not only a soundness, but a readiness of judgment, as men do by the same methods on all other occasions.

SAMUEL JOHNSON (1709–84): from *Rasselas* (1759) and the preface to Shakespeare (1765)

Poetry and Truth to Nature

The business of a poet, said Imlac, is to examine, not the individual, but the species; to remark general properties and large appearances. He does not number the streaks of the tulip, or describe the different shades in the verdure of the forest: he is to exhibit in his portraits of Nature such prominent and striking features, as recall the original to every mind; and must neglect the minuter discriminations, which one may have remarked, and another have neglected, for those characteristics which are alike obvious to vigilance and carelessness.

But the knowledge of Nature is only half the task of a poet: he must be acquainted likewise with all the modes of life. His character requires that he estimate the happiness and misery of every condition, observe the power of all the passions in all their combinations, and trace the changes of the human mind as they are modified by various institutions and accidental influences of climate or custom, from the sprightliness of infancy to the despondence of decrepitude. He must divest himself of the prejudices of his age and country; he must consider right and wrong in their abstracted and invariable state; he must disregard present laws and opinions, and rise to general and transcendental truths, which will always be the same. He must therefore content himself with the slow progress of his name, contemn the applause of his own time, and commit his claims to the justice of posterity. He must write as the interpreter of Nature, and the legislator of mankind, and consider himself as presiding over the thoughts and manners of future generations; as a being superior to time and place.

His labour is not yet at an end; he must know many languages and many sciences; and, that his style may be worthy of his thoughts, must, by incessant practice, familiarise to himself every delicacy of speech and grace of harmony. (*Rasselas*, Chapter X.)

Nothing can please many, and please long, but just representations of general Nature. Particular manners can be known to few, and therefore few only can judge how nearly they are copied. The irregular combinations of fanciful invention may delight awhile, by that novelty of which the common satiety of life sends us all in quest; but the pleasures of sudden wonder are soon exhausted, and the mind can only repose on the stability of truth.

Shakespeare is above all writers, at least above all modern writers, the poet of Nature; the poet that holds up to his readers a faithful mirror of manners and of life. His characters are not modified by the customs of particular places, unpractised by the rest of the world; by the peculiarities of studies or professions, which can operate but upon small numbers; or by the accidents of transient fashions or temporary opinions: they are the genuine progeny of common humanity, such as the world will always supply, and observation will always find. His persons act and speak by the influence of those general passions and principles by which all minds are agitated, and the whole system of life is continued in motion. In the writings of other poets a character is too often an individual; in those of Shakespeare it is commonly a species. (*Preface to Shakespeare*.)

SIR JOSHUA REYNOLDS (1723–92): from *Discourses* (1768–90)

*The Theory of Ideal Beauty. A True Conception of Beauty to be
acquired by the Study of Nature and of Classical Models*

A mere copier of Nature can never produce anything great,
can never raise and enlarge the conceptions, or warm the heart
of the spectator.

The wish of the genuine painter must be more extensive:
instead of endeavouring to amuse mankind with the minute
neatness of his imitations, he must endeavour to improve them
by the grandeur of his ideas; instead of seeking praise, by
deceiving the superficial sense of the spectator, he must strive
for fame by captivating the imagination.

The principle now laid down, that the perfection of this art
does not consist in mere imitation, is far from being new or
singular. It is, indeed, supported by the general opinion of
the enlightened part of mankind. The poets, orators, and
rhetoricians of antiquity, are continually enforcing this
position; that all the arts receive their perfection from an
ideal beauty, superior to what is to be found in individual
nature. They are ever referring to the practice of the painters
and sculptors of their times, particularly Phidias (the favourite
artist of antiquity), to illustrate their assertions. As if they
could not sufficiently express their admiration of his genius by
what they knew, they have recourse to poetical enthusiasm:
they call it inspiration; a gift from Heaven. The artist is
supposed to have ascended the celestial regions, to furnish his
mind with this perfect idea of beauty.

"He," says Proclus, "who takes for his model such forms as
Nature produces, and confines himself to an exact imitation of
them, will never attain to what is perfectly beautiful. For the
works of Nature are full of disproportion, and fall very short
of the true standard of beauty. So that Phidias, when he formed

his Jupiter, did not copy any object ever presented to his sight; but contemplated only that image which he had conceived in his mind from Homer's description." And thus Cicero, speaking of the same Phidias: "Neither did this artist," says he, "when he carved the image of Jupiter or Minerva, set before him any one human figure, as a pattern, which he was to copy; but having a more perfect idea of beauty fixed in his mind, this he steadily contemplated, and to the imitation of this all his skill and labour were directed."

The Moderns are not less convinced than the Ancients of this superior power existing in the art; nor less sensible of its effects. Every language has adopted terms expressive of this excellence. The *gusto grande* of the Italians, the *beau idéal* of the French, and the *great style*, *genius*, and *taste* among the English, are but different appellations of the same thing. It is this intellectual dignity, they say, that ennobles the painter's art; that lays the line between him and the mere mechanic; and produces those great effects in an instant, which eloquence and poetry, by slow and repeated efforts, are scarcely able to attain.

Such is the warmth with which both the Ancients and Moderns speak of this Divine principle of the art; but, as I have formerly observed, enthusiastic admiration seldom promotes knowledge. Though a student by such praise may have his attention roused, and a desire excited, of running in this great career; yet it is possible that what has been said to excite, may only serve to deter him. He examines his own mind, and perceives there nothing of that Divine inspiration, with which, he is told, so many others have been favoured. He never travelled to Heaven to gather new ideas; and he finds himself possessed of no other qualifications than what mere common observation and a plain understanding can confer. Thus he becomes gloomy amidst the splendour of figurative declamation, and thinks it hopeless to pursue an object which he supposes out of the reach of human industry.

But on this, as upon many other occasions, we ought to

distinguish how much is to be given to enthusiasm, and how much to reason. We ought to allow for, and we ought to commend, that strength of vivid expression, which is necessary to convey, in its full force, the highest sense of the most complete effect of art; taking care at the same time, not to lose in terms of vague admiration, that solidity and truth of principle, upon which alone we can reason, and may be enabled to practise.

It is not easy to define in what this great style consists; nor to describe, by words, the proper means of acquiring it, if the mind of the student should be at all capable of such an acquisition. Could we teach taste or genius by rules, they would be no longer taste and genius. But though there neither are, nor can be, any precise invariable rules for the exercise, or the acquisition, of these great qualities, yet we may truly say, that they always operate in proportion to our attention in observing the works of Nature, to our skill in selecting, and to our care in digesting, methodizing, and comparing our observations. There are many beauties in our art, that seem, at first, to lie without the reach of precept, and yet may easily be reduced to practical principles. Experience is all in all; but it is not every one who profits by experience; and most people err, not so much from want of capacity to find their object, as from not knowing what object to pursue. This great ideal perfection and beauty are not to be sought in the heavens, but upon the earth. They are about us, and upon every side of us. But the power of discovering what is deformed in Nature, or in other words, what is particular and uncommon, can be acquired only by experience; and the whole beauty and grandeur of the art consists, in my opinion, in being able to get above all singular forms, local customs, particularities, and details of every kind.

All the objects which are exhibited to our view by Nature, upon close examination will be found to have their blemishes and defects. The most beautiful forms have something about them like weakness, minuteness, or imperfection. But it is not every eye that perceives these blemishes. It must be an eye long used to the contemplation and comparison of these forms; and which by a long habit of observing what any set of objects of the same kind have in common, has acquired the power of discerning what each wants in particular. This long, laborious comparison should be the first study of the painter who aims at the greatest style. By this means, he acquires a just idea of beautiful forms; he corrects Nature by herself, her imperfect state by her more perfect. His eye being enabled to distinguish the accidental deficiencies, excrescences, and deformities of things, from their general figures, he makes out an abstract idea of their forms more perfect than any one original; and what may seem a paradox, he learns to design naturally by drawing his figures unlike to any one object. This idea of the perfect state of Nature, which the artist calls the Ideal Beauty, is the great leading principle by which works of genius are conducted. By this Phidias acquired his fame. He wrought upon a sober principle what has so much excited the enthusiasm of the World. . . .

This is the idea which has acquired, and which seems to have a right to the epithet of *Divine*; as it may be said to preside, like a supreme judge, over all the productions of Nature; appearing to be possessed of the will and intention of the Creator, as far as they regard the external form of living beings. When a man once possesses this idea in its perfection, there is no danger, but that he will be sufficiently warmed by it himself, and be able to warm and ravish every one else.

Thus it is from a reiterated experience, and a close comparison of the objects in Nature, that an artist becomes possessed of the idea of that central form, if I may so express it, from which every deviation is deformity. But the investigation of this form, I grant, is painful, and I know but of one method of shortening the road; this is, by a careful study of the works of the ancient sculptors; who being indefatigable

I

in the school of Nature, have left models of that perfect form behind them, which an artist would prefer as supremely beautiful, who had spent his whole life in that single contemplation. But if industry carried them thus far, may not you also hope for the same reward from the same labour? We have the same school opened to us, that was opened to them; for Nature denies her instructions to none who desire to become her pupils.

This laborious investigation, I am aware, must appear superfluous to those who think everything is to be done by felicity, and the powers of native genius. Even the great Bacon treats with ridicule the idea of confining proportion to rules, or of producing beauty by selection. "A man cannot tell," says he, "whether Apelles or Albert Dürer were the more trifler: whereof the one would make a personage by geometrical proportions; the other, by taking the best parts out of divers faces, to make one excellent. . . . The painter," he adds, "must do it by a kind of felicity, . . . and not by rule."

It is not safe to question any opinion of so great a writer, and so profound a thinker, as undoubtedly Bacon was. But he studies brevity to excess; and therefore his meaning is sometimes doubtful. If he means that beauty has nothing to do with rule, he is mistaken. There is a rule, obtained out of general Nature, to contradict which is to fall into deformity. Whenever anything is done beyond this rule, it is in virtue of some other rule which is followed along with it, but which does not contradict it. Everything which is wrought with certainty, is wrought upon some principle. If it is not, it cannot be repeated. If by felicity is meant any thing of chance or hazard, or something born with a man, and not earned, I cannot agree with this great philosopher. Every object which pleases must give us pleasure upon some certain principles: but as the objects of pleasure are almost infinite, so their principles vary without end, and every man finds them out, not by felicity or successful hazard, but by care and sagacity. (*Discourse III*, December 14, 1770.)

Genius is not opposed to the Rules, but is the Fulfilment of them

For my own part, I confess, I am not only very much disposed to maintain the absolute necessity of imitation in the first stages of the art; but am of opinion that the study of other masters, which I here call imitation, may be extended throughout our whole lives, without any danger of the inconveniences with which it is charged, of enfeebling the mind, or preventing us from giving that original air which every work undoubtedly ought always to have.

I am on the contrary persuaded, that by imitation only, variety, and even originality of invention, is produced. I will go further: even genius, at least what generally is so called, is the child of imitation. But as this appears to be contrary to the general opinion, I must explain my position before I enforce it.

Genius is supposed to be a power of producing excellencies, which are out of the reach of the rules of art; a power which no precepts can teach, and which no industry can acquire. . . .

What we now call genius, begins, not where rules, abstractedly taken, end; but where known vulgar and trite rules have no longer any place. It must of necessity be, that even works of genius, like every other effect, as they must have their cause, must likewise have their rules; it cannot be by chance, that excellencies are produced with any constancy or any certainty, for this is not the nature of chance; but the rules by which men of extraordinary parts, and such as are called men of genius, work, are either such as they discover by their own peculiar observations, or of such a nice texture as not easily to admit being expressed in words; especially as artists are not very frequently skilful in that mode of communicating ideas. Unsubstantial, however, as these rules may seem, and difficult as it may be to convey them in writing, they are still seen and felt in the mind of the artist; and he works from them with as much certainty, as if they were embodied, as I may say, upon paper. It is true, these refined principles cannot be always made palpable, like the more gross rules of art; yet it does not follow, but that the mind may be put in such a train, that it shall perceive, by a kind of scientific sense, that propriety, which words, particularly words of unpractised writers, such as we are, can but very feebly suggest.

Invention is one of the great marks of genius; but if we consult experience, we shall find that it is by being conversant with the inventions of others, that we learn to invent; as by reading the thoughts of others we learn to think. . . .

The mind is but a barren soil; a soil which is soon exhausted, and will produce no crop, or only one, unless it be continually fertilized and enriched with foreign matter.

When we have had continually before us the great works of Art to impregnate our minds with kindred ideas, we are then, and not till then, fit to produce something of the same species. We behold all about us with the eyes of those penetrating observers whose works we contemplate; and our minds, accustomed to think the thoughts of the noblest and brightest intellects, are prepared for the discovery and selection of all that is great and noble in Nature. The greatest natural genius cannot subsist on its own stock: he who resolves never to ransack any mind but his own, will be soon reduced, from mere barrenness, to the poorest of all imitations; he will be obliged to imitate himself and to repeat what he has before often repeated.

.   .   .   .   .

When I speak of the habitual imitation and continued study of masters, it is not to be understood, that I advise any endeavour to copy the exact peculiar colour and complexion of another man's mind; the success of such an attempt must always be like his, who imitates exactly the air, manner, and gestures, of him whom he admires. His model may be excellent, but the copy will be ridiculous; this ridicule does not arise from his having imitated, but from his not having chosen the right mode of imitation. . . .

Nor whilst I recommend studying the art from artists, can I be supposed to mean that Nature is to be neglected; I take this study in aid, and not in exclusion, of the other. Nature is, and must be the fountain which alone is inexhaustible; and from which all excellencies must originally flow.

The great use of studying our predecessors is, to open the mind, to shorten our labour, and to give us the result of the selection made by those great minds of what is grand or beautiful in Nature: her rich stores are all spread out before us; but it is an art, and no easy art, to know how or what to choose, and how to attain and secure the object of our choice. Thus the highest beauty of form must be taken from Nature; but it is an art of long deduction, and great experience, to know how to find it. We must not content ourselves with merely admiring and relishing; we must enter into the principles on which the work is wrought: these do not swim on the superficies, and consequently are not open to superficial observers.

Art in its perfection is not ostentatious; it lies hid, and works its effect, itself unseen. It is the proper study and labour of an artist to uncover and find out the latent cause of conspicuous beauties, and from thence form principles of his own conduct: such an examination is a continual exertion of the mind; as great, perhaps, as that of the artist whose works he is thus studying. (*Discourse VI*, December 10, 1774.)

Taste and Genius are not Independent of Reason and Experience, because they are founded on Truth to Nature

It has been the fate of arts to be enveloped in mysterious and incomprehensible language, as if it was thought necessary that even the terms should correspond to the idea entertained of the instability and uncertainty of the rules which they expressed.

To speak of genius and taste as in any way connected with reason or common sense, would be, in the opinion of some towering talkers, to speak like a man who possessed neither; who had never felt that enthusiasm, or, to use their own inflated language, was never warmed by that Promethean fire, which animates the canvas and vivifies the marble.

If, in order to be intelligible, I appear to degrade art by bringing her down from her visionary situation in the clouds, it is only to give her a more solid mansion upon the earth. It is necessary that at some time or other we should see things as they really are, and not impose on ourselves by that false magnitude with which objects appear when viewed indistinctly as through a mist. . . .

Genius and taste, in their common acceptation, appear to be very nearly related; the difference lies only in this, that genius has superadded to it a habit or power of execution: or we may say, that taste, when this power is added, changes its name, and is called genius. They both, in the popular opinion, pretend to an entire exemption from the restraint of rules. It is supposed that their powers are intuitive; that under the name of genius great works are produced, and under the name of taste an exact judgment is given, without our knowing why, and without our being under the least obligation to reason, precept, or experience.

One can scarce state these opinions without exposing their absurdity; yet they are constantly in the mouths of men, and particularly of artists. They who have thought seriously on this subject, do not carry the point so far; yet I am persuaded that even among those few who may be called thinkers, the prevalent opinion allows less than it ought to the powers of reason; and considers the principles of taste, which give all their authority to the rules of art, as more fluctuating, and as having less solid foundations, than we shall find, upon examination, they really have.

The common saying, that *tastes are not to be disputed*, owes its influence, and its general reception, to the same error which leads us to imagine this faculty of too high an original to submit to the authority of an earthly tribunal. It likewise corresponds with the notions of those who consider it as a mere phantom of the imagination, so devoid of substance as to elude all criticism. . . .

Of the judgment which we make on the works of art, and the preference that we give to one class of art over another, if a reason be demanded, the question is perhaps evaded by answering, 'I judge from my taste.' But it does not follow that a better answer cannot be given, though, for common gazers, this may be sufficient. Every man is not obliged to investigate the causes of his approbation or dislike.

The arts would lie open for ever to caprice and casualty, if those who are to judge of their excellencies had no settled principles by which they are to regulate their decisions, and the merit or defect of performances were to be determined by unguided fancy. And indeed we may venture to assert, that whatever speculative knowledge is necessary to the artist, is equally and indispensably necessary to the connoisseur.

The first idea that occurs in the consideration of what is fixed in art, or in taste, is that presiding principle of which I have so frequently spoken in former discourses—the general idea of Nature. The beginning, the middle, and the end of everything that is valuable in taste, is comprised in the knowledge of what is truly Nature; for whatever notions are not conformable to those of Nature, or universal opinion, must be considered as more or less capricious.

My notion of Nature comprehends not only the forms which Nature produces, but also the nature and internal fabric and organization, as I may call it, of the human mind and imagination. The terms beauty, or Nature, which are general ideas, are but different modes of expressing the same thing, whether we apply these terms to statues, poetry, or pictures. Deformity is not Nature, but an accidental deviation from her accustomed practice. This general idea therefore ought to be called Nature;

and nothing else, correctly speaking, has a right to that name. But we are so far from speaking, in common conversation, with any such accuracy, that, on the contrary, when we criticise Rembrandt and other Dutch painters, who introduced into their historical pictures exact representations of individual objects with all their imperfections, we say 'Though it is not in a good taste, yet it is Nature.'

This misapplication of terms must be very often perplexing to the young student. Is not art, he may say, an imitation of Nature? Must he not therefore who imitates her with the greatest fidelity, be the best artist? By this mode of reasoning Rembrandt has a higher place than Raffaelle. But a very little reflection will serve to show us, that these particularities cannot be Nature: for how can that be the nature of man, in which no two individuals are the same?

It plainly appears, that as a work is conducted under the influence of general ideas, or partial, it is principally to be considered as the effect of a good or a bad taste.

As beauty, therefore, does not consist in taking what lies immediately before you, so neither, in our pursuit of taste, are those opinions which we first received and adopted, the best choice, or the most natural to the mind and imagination. In the infancy of our knowledge we seize with greediness the good that is within our reach; it is by after-consideration, and in consequence of discipline, that we refuse the present for a greater good at a distance. The nobility or elevation of all arts, like the excellency of virtue itself, consists in adopting this enlarged and comprehensive idea; and all criticism built upon the more confined view of what is natural, may properly be called *shallow* criticism, rather than false; its defect is, that the truth is not sufficiently extensive. . . .

The poet and actor, as well as the painter of genius who is well acquainted with all the variety and sources of pleasure in the mind and imagination, has little regard or attention to common Nature, or creeping after common sense. By overleaping those narrow bounds, he more effectually seizes the whole mind, and more powerfully accomplishes his purpose. This success is ignorantly imagined to proceed from inattention to all rules, and a defiance of reason and judgment; whereas it is in truth acting according to the best rules and the justest reason.

He who thinks Nature, in the narrow sense of the word, is alone to be followed, will produce but a scanty entertainment for the imagination: every thing is to be done with which it is natural for the mind to be pleased, whether it proceeds from simplicity or variety, uniformity or irregularity; whether the scenes are familiar or exotic; rude and wild, or enriched and cultivated; for it is natural for the mind to be pleased with all these in their turn. In short, whatever pleases has in it what is analogous to the mind, and is therefore, in the highest and best sense of the word, natural.

It is the sense of Nature or truth, which ought more particularly to be cultivated by the professors of art; and it may be observed, that many wise and learned men, who have accustomed their minds to admit nothing for truth but what can be proved by mathematical demonstration, have seldom any relish for those arts which address themselves to the fancy, the rectitude and truth of which is known by another kind of proof: and we may add, that the acquisition of this knowledge requires as much circumspection and sagacity, as is necessary to attain those truths which are more capable of demonstration. Reason must ultimately determine our choice on every occasion; but this reason may still be exerted ineffectually by applying to taste principles which, though right as far as they go, yet do not reach the object. No man, for instance, can deny, that it seems at first view very reasonable, that a statue which is to carry down to posterity the resemblance of an individual, should be dressed in the fashion of the times, in the dress which himself wore: this would certainly be true, if the dress were part of the man: but after a time, the dress is only an amusement for an antiquarian; and if it obstructs the general design of the piece, it is to be disregarded by the artist. Common sense must here give way to a higher sense. In the naked form, and in the disposition of the drapery, the difference between one artist and another is principally seen. But if he is compelled to exhibit the modern dress, the naked form is entirely hid, and the drapery is already disposed by the skill of the tailor. Were a Phidias to obey such absurd commands, he would please no more than an ordinary sculptor; since, in the inferior parts of every art, the learned and the ignorant are nearly upon a level.

．　　．　　．　　．　　．

By these considerations, which can never be too frequently impressed, may be obviated two errors, which I observed to have been, formerly at least, the most prevalent, and to be most injurious to artists; that of thinking taste and genius to have nothing to do with reason, and that of taking particular living objects for nature.

I shall now say something on that part of *taste*, which, as I have hinted to you before, does not belong so much to the external form of things, but is addressed to the mind, and depends on its original frame, or, to use the expression, the organization of the soul; I mean the imagination and the passions. The principles of these are as invariable as the former, and are to be known and reasoned upon in the same manner, by an appeal to common sense deciding upon the common feelings of mankind. This sense, and these feelings, appear to me of equal authority, and equally conclusive. Now this appeal implies a general uniformity and agreement in the minds of men. It would be else an idle and vain endeavour to establish rules of art; it would be pursuing a phantom, to attempt to move affections with which we were entirely unacquainted. We have no reason to suspect there is a greater difference between our minds than between our forms; of which, though there are no two alike, yet there is a general similitude that goes through the whole race of mankind; and those who have cultivated their taste, can distinguish what is beautiful or deformed, or, in other words, what agrees with or deviates from the general idea of Nature, in one case, as well as in the other.

The internal fabric of our minds, as well as the external form of our bodies, being nearly uniform, it seems then to follow of course, that as the imagination is incapable of producing anything originally of itself, and can only vary and combine those ideas with which it is furnished by means of the senses, there will be necessarily an agreement in the imaginations, as in the senses of men. There being this agreement, it follows, that in all cases, in our lightest amusements, as well as in our most serious actions and engagements of life, we must regulate our affections of every kind by that of others. The well-disciplined mind acknowledges this authority, and submits its own opinion to the public voice. It is from knowing what are the general feelings and passions of mankind, that we acquire a true idea of what imagination is; though it appears as if we had nothing to do but to consult our own particular sensations, and these were sufficient to ensure us from all error and mistake.

A knowledge of the disposition and character of the human mind can be acquired only by experience; a great deal will be learned, I admit, by a habit of examining what passes in our bosoms, what are our own motives of action, and of what kind of sentiments we are conscious on any occasion. We may suppose an uniformity, and conclude that the same effect will be produced by the same cause in the minds of others. This examination will contribute to suggest to us matters of enquiry; but we can never be sure that our own sentiments are true and right, till they are confirmed by more extensive observation. One man opposing another determines nothing; but a general union of minds, like a general combination of the forces of all mankind, makes a strength that is irresistible. In fact, as he who does not know himself, does not know others, so it may be said with equal truth, that he who does not know others, knows himself but very imperfectly.

A man who thinks he is guarding himself against prejudices by resisting the authority of others, leaves open every avenue to singularity, vanity, self-conceit, obstinacy, and many other vices, all tending to warp the judgment, and prevent the natural operation of his faculties. This submission to others is a deference which we owe, and indeed are forced involuntarily to pay. In fact, we never are satisfied with our opinions, whatever we may pretend, till they are ratified and confirmed by the suffrages of the rest of mankind. We dispute and wrangle for ever; we endeavour to get men to come to us, when we do not go to them.

He therefore who is acquainted with the works which have pleased different ages and different countries, and has formed his opinion on them, has more materials, and more means of knowing what is analogous to the mind of man, than he who is conversant only with the works of his own age or country. What has pleased, and continues to please, is likely to please again: hence are derived the rules of art, and on this immovable foundation they must ever stand.

This search and study of the history of the mind ought not to be confined to one art only. It is by the analogy that one art bears to another, that many things are ascertained, which either were but faintly seen, or, perhaps, would not have been discovered at all, if the inventor had not received the first hints from the practices of a sister art on a similar occasion. The frequent allusions which every man who treats of any art is obliged to make to others, in order to illustrate and confirm his principles, sufficiently show their near connection and inseparable relation.

All arts having the same general end, which is to please; and addressing themselves to the same faculties through the medium of the senses; it follows that their rules and principles must have as great affinity, as the different materials and the different organs or vehicles by which they pass to the mind, will permit them to retain.

We may therefore conclude, that the real substance, as it may be called, of what goes under the name of taste, is fixed and established in the nature of things; that there are certain and regular causes by which the imagination and passions of men are affected; and that the knowledge of these causes is acquired by a laborious and diligent investigation of Nature, and by the same slow progress as wisdom or knowledge of every kind, however instantaneous its operations may appear when thus acquired.

It has been often observed, that the good and virtuous man alone can acquire this true or just relish even of works of art. This opinion will not appear entirely without foundation, when we consider that the same habit of mind which is acquired by our search after truth in the more serious duties of life, is only transferred to the pursuit of lighter amusements. The same disposition, the same desire to find something steady, substantial, and durable, on which the mind can lean as it were, and rest with safety, actuates us in both cases. The subject only is changed. We pursue the same method in our search after the idea of beauty and perfection in each; of virtue, by looking forwards beyond ourselves to society, and to the whole; of arts, by extending our views in the same manner to all ages and all times.

Every art, like our own, has in its composition fluctuating as well as fixed principles. It is an attentive enquiry into their difference that will enable us to determine how far we are influenced by custom and habit, and what is fixed in the nature of things.

To distinguish how much has solid foundation, we may have recourse to the same proof by which some hold that wit ought to be tried: whether it preserves itself when translated. That wit is false, which can subsist only in one language; and that picture which pleases only one age or one nation, owes its reception to some local or accidental association of ideas. (*Discourse VII*, December 10, 1776.)

V. *THE IDEA OF HISTORICAL CRITICISM*

ALEXANDER POPE (1688–1744): from the preface to Shakespeare
(1725)

Shakespeare and his Age

It must be allowed that stage-poetry of all other is more
particularly levelled to please the populace, and its success
more immediately depending upon the common suffrage. One
cannot therefore wonder, if Shakespeare, having at his first
appearance no other aim in his writings than to procure a
subsistence, directed his endeavours solely to hit the taste and
humour that then prevailed. The audience was generally
composed of the meaner sort of people; and therefore the
images of life were to be drawn from those of their own rank.
Accordingly we find that not our author's only but almost all
the old comedies have their scene among tradesmen and
mechanics; and even their historical plays strictly follow the
common old stories or vulgar traditions of that kind of people.
In tragedy, nothing was so sure to surprise and cause admiration, as the most strange, unexpected, and consequently most
unnatural, events and incidents; the most exaggerated
thoughts; the most verbose and bombast expression; the most
pompous rhymes, and thundering versification. In comedy,
nothing was so sure to please, as mean buffoonery, vile ribaldry,
and unmannerly jests of fools and clowns. . . .

It may be added, that not only the common audience had
no notion of the rules of writing, but few even of the better
sort piqued themselves upon any great degree of knowledge or

nicety that way, till Ben Jonson getting possession of the stage brought critical learning into vogue: and that this was not done without difficulty, may appear from those frequent lessons (and indeed almost declamations) which he was forced to prefix to his first plays, and put into the mouth of his actors, the *Grex*, *Chorus*, etc., to remove the prejudices, and inform the judgment of his hearers. Till then, our authors had no thoughts of writing on the model of the Ancients: their tragedies were only histories in dialogue; and their comedies followed the thread of any novel as they found it, no less implicitly than if it had been true history.

To judge therefore of Shakespeare by Aristotle's rules, is like trying a man by the laws of one country, who acted under those of another. He wrote to the people; and wrote at first without patronage from the better sort, and therefore without aims of pleasing them; without assistance or advice from the learned, as without the advantage of education or acquaintance among them; without that knowledge of the best models, the Ancients, to inspire him with an emulation of them; in a word, without any views of reputation, and of what poets are pleased to call immortality—some or all of which have encouraged the vanity, or animated the ambition, of other writers. . . .

I will conclude by saying of Shakespeare, that with all his faults, and with all the irregularity of his drama, one may look upon his works, in comparison of those that are more finished and regular, as upon an ancient, majestic piece of Gothic architecture, compared with a neat modern building. The latter is more elegant and glaring, but the former is more strong and more solemn. It must be allowed that in one of these there are materials enough to make many of the other. It has much the greater variety, and much the nobler apartments; though we are often conducted to them by dark, odd, and uncouth passages. Nor does the whole fail to strike us with greater reverence, though many of the parts are childish, ill-placed, and unequal to its grandeur.

RICHARD HURD (1720–1808): from *Letters on Chivalry and Romance* (1762)

A Defence of Romantic Literature

But nothing shows the difference of the two systems under consideration more plainly, than the effect they really had on the two greatest of our poets; at least the two which an English reader is most fond to compare with Homer, I mean Spenser and Milton.

It is not to be doubted but that each of these bards had kindled his poetic fire from classic fables. So that, of course, their prejudices would lie that way. Yet they both appear, when most inflamed, to have been more particularly rapt with the Gothic fables of chivalry.

Spenser, though he had been long nourished with the spirit and substance of Homer and Virgil, chose the times of chivalry for his theme, and Fairy Land for the scene of his fictions. He could have planned, no doubt, an heroic design on the exact classic model: or, he might have trimmed between the Gothic and Classic, as his contemporary Tasso did. But the charms of *fairy* prevailed. And if any think, he was seduced by Ariosto into this choice, they should consider that it could be only for the sake of his subject; for the genius and character of these poets was widely different.

Under this idea then of a Gothic, not classical poem, the *Faery Queen* is to be read and criticized. And on these principles, it would not be difficult to unfold its merit in another way than has been hitherto attempted.

Milton, it is true, preferred the classic model to the Gothic. But it was after long hesitation; and his favourite subject was *Arthur and his Knights of the Round Table*. On this he had fixed for the greater part of his life. What led him to change his mind was, partly, as I suppose, his growing fanaticism; partly, his ambition to take a different route from Spenser; but chiefly perhaps, the discredit into which the stories of chivalry had now fallen by the immortal satire of Cervantes. Yet we see through all his poetry, where his enthusiasm flames out most, a certain predilection for the legends of chivalry before the fables of Greece.

This circumstance, you know, has given offence to the austerer and more mechanical critics. They are ready to censure his judgment, as juvenile and unformed, when they see him so delighted, on all occasions, with the Gothic romances. But do these censors imagine that Milton did not perceive the defects of these works, as well as they? No: it was not the *composition* of books of chivalry, but the *manners* described in them, that took his fancy; as appears from his *Allegro*:

> Towred cities please us then
> And the busy hum of men,
> Where throngs of knights and barons bold
> In weeds of peace high triumphs hold,
> With store of ladies, whose bright eyes
> Rain influence, and judge the prize
> Of wit, or arms, while both contend
> To win her grace, whom all commend.

And when in the *Penseroso* he draws, by a fine contrivance, the same kind of image to soothe melancholy which he had before given to excite mirth, he indeed extols an *author* of one of these romances, as he had before, in general, extolled the *subject* of them; but it is an author worthy of his praise; not the writer of *Amadis*, or *Sir Launcelot of the Lake*, but Chaucer himself, who has left an unfinished story on the Gothic or feudal model.

> Or, call up him that left half-told
> The story of Cambuscan bold,
> Of Camball and of Algarsife,
> And who had Canace to wife
> That own'd the virtuous ring and glass,
> And of the wondrous horse of brass,

K

On which the Tartar king did ride;
And if ought else great bards beside
In sage and solemn tunes have sung
Of turneys and of trophies hung,
Of forests and inchantments drear,
Where more is meant than meets the ear.

The conduct, then, of these two poets may incline us to think with more respect than is commonly done of the *Gothic manners*, I mean as adapted to the uses of the greater poetry.

I say nothing of Shakespeare, because the sublimity (the divinity, let it be, if nothing else will serve) of his genius kept no certain route, but rambled at hazard into all the regions of human life and manners. So that we can hardly say what he preferred, or what he rejected, on full deliberation. Yet one thing is clear, that even he is greater when he uses Gothic manners and machinery, than when he employs classical: which brings us again to the same point, that the former have, by their nature and genius, the advantage of the latter in producing the *sublime*. (Letter VII.)

The Classical Rules Inapplicable to Works belonging to the Romantic Tradition

I spoke " of criticizing Spenser's poem, under the idea, not of a classical but Gothic composition."

It is certain much light might be thrown on that singular work, were an able critic to consider it in this view. For instance, he might go some way towards explaining, perhaps justifying, the general plan and *conduct* of the *Faery Queen*, which, to classical readers, has appeared indefensible. . . .

When an architect examines a Gothic structure by Grecian rules, he finds nothing but deformity. But the Gothic architecture has its own rules, by which when it comes to be examined, it is seen to have its merit, as well as the Grecian. The question is not, which of the two is conducted in the simplest or truest taste; but, whether there be not sense and design in both, when scrutinized by the laws on which each is projected.

The same observation holds of the two sorts of poetry. Judge of the *Faery Queen* by the classic models, and you are shocked with its disorder: consider it with an eye to its Gothic original, and you find it regular. The unity and simplicity of the former are more complete: but the latter has that sort of unity and simplicity, which results from its nature.

The *Faery Queen* then, as a Gothic poem, derives its *method*, as well as the other characters of its composition, from the established modes and ideas of chivalry.

It was usual, in the days of knight-errantry, at the holding of any great feast, for Knights to appear before the Prince, who presided at it, and claim the privilege of being sent on any adventure, to which the solemnity might give occasion. For it was supposed that, when such a "throng of knights and barons bold," as Milton speaks of, were got together, the distressed would flock in from all quarters, as to a place where they knew they might find and claim redress for all their grievances.

This was the real practice, in the days of pure and ancient chivalry. And an image of this practice was afterwards kept up in the castles of the great, on any extraordinary festival or solemnity: of which, if you want an instance, I refer you to the description of a feast made at Lisle in 1453, in the court of Philip the Good, Duke of Burgundy, for a crusade against the Turks: as you may find it given at large in the memoirs of Matthieu de Couci, Olivier de la Marche, and Monstrelet.

That feast was held for *twelve* days: and each day was distinguished by the claim and allowance of some adventure.

Now, laying down this practice as a foundation for the poet's design, you will see how properly the *Faery Queen* is conducted.

"I devise," says the poet himself in his Letter to Sir W. Raleigh, "that the Faery Queen kept her annual feaste xii days: upon which xii several days, the occasions of the xii several adventures hapened; which being undertaken by xii several knights, are in these xii books severally handled."

Here you have the poet delivering his own method, and the reason of it. It arose out of the order of his subject. And would you desire a better reason for his choice? . . . It was as requisite for the *Faery Queen* to consist of the adventures of twelve knights, as for the *Odyssey* to be confined to the adventures of one hero: justice had otherwise not been done to his subject.

So that if you will say anything against the poet's method, you must say that he should not have chosen this subject. But this objection arises from your classic ideas of Unity, which have no place here; and are in every view foreign to the purpose, if the poet has found means to give his work, though consisting of many parts, the advantage of unity. For in some reasonable sense or other, it is agreed, every work of art must be *one*, the very idea of a work requiring it.

If you ask then, what is this *unity* of Spenser's poem, I say it consists in the relation of its several adventures to one common *original*, the appointment of the Faery Queen; and to one common *end*, the completion of the Faery Queen's injunctions. The knights issued forth on their adventures on the breaking up of this annual feast; and the next annual feast, we are to suppose, is to bring them together again from the achievement of their several charges.

This, it is true, is not the classic unity, which consists in the representation of one entire action: but it is an unity of another sort, an unity resulting from the respect which a number of related actions have to one common purpose. In other words, it is an unity of *design*, and not of action.

This Gothic method of design in poetry may be, in some sort, illustrated by what is called the Gothic method of design in gardening. A wood or grove cut out into many separate avenues or glades was amongst the most favourite of the works of art which our fathers attempted in this species of cultivation. These walks were distinct from each other, had, each, their several destination, and terminated on their own proper objects. Yet the whole was brought together and considered under one view by the relation which these various openings had, not to each other, but to their common and concurrent centre. You and I are, perhaps, agreed that this sort of gardening is not of so true a taste as that which Kent and Nature have brought us acquainted with; where the supreme art of the Designer consists in disposing his ground and objects into an *entire landscape*; and grouping them, if I may use the term, in so easy a manner, that the careless observer, though he be taken with the symmetry of the whole, discovers no art in the combination:

> In lieto aspetto il bel giardin s'aperse,
> Acque stagnanti, mobili cristalli,
> Fior vari, e varie piante, herbe diverse,
> Apriche Collinette, ombrose valli,
> Selve, e spelunche in UNA VISTA offerse:
> E quel, che'l bello, e'l caro accresce à l'opre,
> L'Arte, che tutto fà, nulla si scopre.
>
> TASSO. C. xvi. S. ix

This, I say, may be the truest taste in gardening, because the simplest. Yet there is a manifest regard to unity in the other method; which has had its admirers, as it may have again, and is certainly not without its *design* and beauty. (Letter VIII.)

Lord Shaftesbury (1671–1713): from *Characteristics* (1709)

Primitive Nature

O glorious Nature! supremely fair and sovereignly good! all-loving and all-lovely, all-divine! . . . whose every single work affords an ampler scene and is a nobler spectacle than all which art ever presented! . . . I shall no longer resist the passion growing in me for things of a *natural* kind; where neither art, nor the conceit or caprice of man has spoiled that genuine order, by breaking in upon that primitive state. Even the rude rocks, the mossy caverns, the irregular, unwrought grottoes and the broken falls of waters, with all the horrid graces of the wilderness itself, as representing Nature more, will be the more engaging and appear with a magnificence beyond the mockery of princely gardens.

Joseph Addison (1672–1719): from *The Spectator*, No. 414 (1712)

Artificial and Natural Gardens

We have before observed that there is generally in Nature something more grand and august, than what we meet with in the curiosities of Art. When, therefore, we see this imitated in any measure, it gives us a nobler and more exalted kind of pleasure than what we receive from the nicer and more accurate productions of Art. On this account our English gardens are not so entertaining to the fancy as those in France and Italy, where we see a large extent of ground covered over with an agreeable mixture of garden and forest, which represent everywhere an artificial rudeness, much more charming than that neatness and elegance which we meet with in those of our own country. It might, indeed, be of ill consequence to the public, as well as unprofitable to private persons, to alienate so much ground from pasturage and the plough, in many parts of a country that is so well peopled, and cultivated to a far greater advantage. But why may not a whole estate be thrown into a kind of garden by frequent plantations, that may turn as much to the profit as the pleasure of the owner? A marsh overgrown with willows, or a mountain shaded with oaks, are not only more beautiful, but more beneficial, than when they lie bare and unadorned. Fields of corn make a pleasant prospect, and if the walks were a little taken care of that lie between them, if the natural embroidery of the meadows were helped and improved by some small additions of art, and the several rows of hedges set off by trees and flowers, that the soil was capable of receiving, a man might make a pretty landscape of his own possessions.

Writers who have given us an account of China, tell us the inhabitants of that country laugh at the plantations of our Europeans which are laid out by the rule and line; because, they say, anyone may place trees in equal rows and uniform figures. They choose rather to show a genius in works of this nature, and therefore always conceal the art by which they direct themselves. They have a word, it seems, in their language, by which they express the particular beauty of a plantation that thus strikes the imagination at first sight, without discovering what it is that has so agreeable an effect. Our British gardeners, on the contrary, instead of humouring Nature, love to deviate from it as much as possible. Our trees rise in cones, globes and pyramids. We see the marks of the scissors upon every plant and bush. I do not know whether I am singular in my opinion, but, for my own part, I would rather look upon a tree in all its luxuriancy and diffusion of boughs and branches, than when it is thus cut and trimmed into a mathematical figure; and cannot but fancy that an orchard in flower looks infinitely more delightful than all the little labyrinths of the most finished parterre. But as our great modellers of gardens have their magazines of plants to dispose of, it is very natural for them to tear up all the beautiful plantations of fruit trees, and contrive a plan that may most turn to their own profit, in taking off their evergreens, and the like movable plants, with which their shops are plentifully stocked.

HORACE WALPOLE (1717–97): from his *Letters*

Sublimity in Nature

But the road, West, the road! winding round a prodigious mountain, and surrounded with others, all shagged with hanging woods, obscured with pines, or lost in clouds! Below, a torrent breaking through cliffs, and tumbling through fragments of rocks! Sheets of cascades forcing their silver speed down channelled precipices, and hasting into the roughened river at the bottom! Now and then an old foot-bridge, with a broken rail, a leaning cross, a cottage, or the ruin of an hermitage! This sounds too bombast and too romantic to one that has not seen it, too cold for one that has. If I could send you my letter post between two lovely tempests that echoed each other's wrath, you might have some idea of this noble roaring scene, as you were reading it. Almost on the summit, upon a fine verdure, but without any prospect, stands the Chartreuse. (From a letter to Richard West, from a hamlet among the mountains of Savoy, Sept. 28, 1739.)

THOMAS GRAY (1716–71): from his *Letters*

The Grande Chartreuse

... It is a fortnight since we set out from hence upon a little excursion to Geneva. We took the longest road, which lies through Savoy, on purpose to see a famous monastery, called the Grande Chartreuse, and had no reason to think our time lost. After having travelled seven days very slow (for we did not change horses, it being impossible for a chaise to go post in these roads) we arrived at a little village, among the mountains of Savoy, called Echelles; from thence we proceeded on horses, who are used to the way, to the mountain of the Chartreuse. It is six miles to the top; the road runs winding up it, commonly not six feet broad; on one hand is the rock, with woods of pine-trees hanging overhead; on the other a monstrous precipice, almost perpendicular, at the bottom of which rolls a torrent, that sometimes tumbling among the fragments of stone that have fallen from on high, and sometimes precipitating itself down vast descents with a noise like thunder, which is still made greater by the echo from the mountains on each side, concurs to form one of the most solemn, the most romantic, and the most astonishing scenes I ever beheld. Add to this the strange views made by the crags and cliffs on the other hand; the cascades that in many places throw themselves from the very summit down into the vale, and the river below; and many other particulars impossible to describe; you will conclude we had no occasion to repent our pains. (From a letter to his mother, written from Lyons, October 13, 1739.)

... I own I have not, as yet, anywhere met with those grand and simple works of art that are to amaze one, and whose sight one is to be the better for; but those of Nature have astonished me beyond expression. In our little journey up to the Grande Chartreuse, I do not remember to have gone ten paces without an exclamation that there was no restraining: not a precipice, not a torrent, not a cliff, but is pregnant with religion and poetry. There are certain scenes that would awe an atheist into belief, without the help of other argument. One need not have a very fantastic imagination to see spirits there at noon-day. You have Death perpetually before your eyes, only so far removed as to compose the mind without frighting it. I am well persuaded St Bruno was a man of no common genius to choose such a situation for his retirement, and perhaps should have been a disciple of his, had I been born in his time. (From a letter to Richard West, November 16, 1739.)

Netley Abbey, Southampton

I received your letter before I left London, and sit down to write to you, after the finest walk in the finest day that ever shone to Netley Abbey—my old friend, with whom I longed to renew my acquaintance. My ferryman (for one passes over a little arm of the sea about half a mile) assured me he would not go near it in the night-time for all the world, though he knew much money had been found there. The sun was "all too glaring and too full of gauds" for such a scene, which ought to be visited only in the dusk of the evening. It stands in a little quiet valley, which gradually rises behind the ruins into a half-circle crowned with thick wood. Before it, on a descent, is a thicket of oaks, that serves to veil it from the broad day and from profane eyes, only leaving a peep on both sides, where the sea appears glittering through the shade, and vessels with their white sails, that glide across and are lost again. Concealed behind the thicket stands a little castle (also in ruins) immediately on the shore, that commands a view over an expanse of sea clear and smooth as glass (when I saw it), with Southampton and several villages three miles off to the

right, Calshot Castle at seven miles' distance, and the high
lands of the Isle of Wight to the left, and in front the deep
shades of the New Forest distinctly seen, because the water is
no more than three miles over. The abbey was never very
large. The shell of its church is almost entire, but the pillars of
the aisles are gone, and the roof has tumbled in; yet some little
of it is left in the transept, where the ivy has forced its way
through, and hangs flaunting down among the fretted ornament and the escutcheons of the Benefactors. Much of the
lodgings and offices are also standing, but all is overgrown with
trees and bushes, and mantled here and there with ivy, that
mounts over the battlements. (From a letter to the Reverend
James Brown, October 1764)

The English Lakes

Oct: 3. Wind at S:E:; a heavenly day. Rose at seven, and
walked out under the conduct of my landlord to Borrowdale.
The grass was covered with a hoar-frost, which soon melted
and exhaled in a thin bluish smoke. Crossed the meadows
obliquely, catching a diversity of views among the hills over
the lake and islands, and changing prospect at every ten paces,
left Cockshut and Castle-hill behind me, and drew near the
foot of Walla-crag, whose bare and rocky brow, cut perpen-
dicularly down above four hundred feet, as I guess, awfully
overlooks the way. Our path here tends to the left, and the
ground gently rising, and covered with a glade of scattering
trees and bushes on the very margin of the water, opens both
ways the most delicious view that my eyes ever beheld. Behind
you are the magnificent heights of Walla-crag; opposite lie the
thick hanging woods of Lord Egremont, and Newland valley,
with green and smiling fields embosomed in the dark cliffs; to the
left the jaws of Borrowdale, with that turbulent chaos of
mountain behind mountain rolled in confusion; beneath you,
and stretching far away to the right, the shining purity of the

lake, just ruffled by the breeze enough to show it is alive,
reflecting rocks, woods, fields, and inverted tops of mountains,
with the white buildings of Keswick, Crosthwaite church,
and Skiddaw for a background at a distance. Oh Doctor! I
never wished more for you; and pray think, how the glass
played its part in such a spot, which is called Carf Close Reeds.
I choose to set down these barbarous names, that anybody
may enquire on the place and easily find the particular station
that I mean. This scene continues to Barrow-gate, and a little
farther, passing a brook called Barrow-beck, we entered
Borrowdale. The crags, named Lodore-banks, now begin to
impend terribly over your way; and more terribly, when you
hear, that three years since an immense mass of rock tumbled
at once from the brow, and barred all access to the dale (for
this is the only road) till they could work their way through it.
Luckily no one was passing at the time of this fall; but down
the side of the mountain, and far into the lake, lie dispersed the
huge fragments of this ruin, in all shapes and in all directions.
Something farther we turned aside into a coppice, ascending a
little in front of Lodore waterfall. The height appears to be
about two hundred feet, the quantity of water not great,
though (these three days excepted) it had rained daily in the
hills for near two months before; but then the stream was
nobly broken, leaping from rock to rock, and foaming with
fury. On one side a towering crag, that spired up to equal, if
not overtop, the neighbouring cliffs (this lay all in shade and
darkness). On the other hand a rounder, broader, projecting
hill shagged with wood and illumined by the sun, which
glanced sideways on the upper part of the cataract. The force
of the water, wearing a deep channel in the ground, hurries
away to join the lake. We descended again, and passed the
stream over a rude bridge. Soon after we came under Gowder-
crag, a hill more formidable to the eye and to the apprehension
than that of Lodore; the rocks atop, deep-cloven perpen-
dicularly by the rains, hanging loose and nodding forwards,

seem just starting from their base in shivers; the whole way
down, and the road on both sides, is strewn with piles of
fragments strangely thrown across each other and of a dreadful
bulk. The place reminds one of those passes in the Alps,
where the Guides tell you to move on with speed, and
say nothing, lest the agitation of the air should loosen the
snows above, and bring down a mass, that would over-
whelm a caravan. I took their counsel here and hastened on
in silence.

·   ·   ·   ·   ·

Walked leisurely home the way we came, but saw a new
landscape: the features indeed were the same in part, but many
new ones were disclosed by the mid-day sun, and the tints
were entirely changed. Take notice this was the best or perhaps
the only day for going up Skiddaw, but I thought it better
employed: it was perfectly serene, and hot as Midsummer.
In the evening walked alone down to the lake by the side of
Crow-Park after sunset, and saw the solemn colouring of light
draw on, the last gleam of sunshine fading away on the hilltops,
the deep serene of the waters, and the long shadows of the
mountains thrown across them, till they nearly touched the
hithermost shore. At distance heard the murmur of many
waterfalls, not audible in the day-time. Wished for the Moon,
but she was *dark to me and silent, hid in her vacant interlunar cave.*
(From his journal-letter to Dr Wharton, 1769.)

HORACE WALPOLE (1717–97): from *History of the Modern Taste
in Gardening* (1771)

The Formal Garden of the Seventeenth Century

When the custom of making square gardens enclosed with
walls was thus established, to the exclusion of Nature and

prospect,[1] pomp and solitude combined to call for something that might enrich and enliven the insipid and unanimated partition. Fountains, first invented for use, which grandeur loves to disguise and throw out of the question, received embellishments from costly marbles, and at last to contradict utility, tossed their waste of waters into air in spouting columns. Art, in the hands of rude man, had at first been made a succedaneum to Nature; in the hands of ostentatious wealth, it became the means of opposing Nature; and the more it traversed the march of the latter, the more nobility thought its power was demonstrated. Canals measured by the line were introduced in lieu of meandering streams, and terraces were hoisted aloft in opposition to the facile slopes that imperceptibly unite the valley to the hill. Balustrades defended these precipitate and dangerous elevations, and flights of steps rejoined them to the subjacent flat from which the terrace had been dug. Vases and sculpture were added to these unnecessary balconies, and statues furnished the lifeless spot with mimic representations of the excluded sons of men. Thus difficulty and expense were the constituent parts of those sumptuous and selfish solitudes; and every improvement that was made, was but a step farther from Nature. The tricks of waterworks to wet the unwary, not to refresh the panting spectator, and parterres embroidered in patterns like a petticoat, were but the childish endeavours of fashion and novelty to reconcile greatness to what it had surfeited on. To crown these impotent displays of false taste, the shears were applied to the lovely wildness of form with which Nature has distinguished each various species of tree and shrub. The venerable oak, the romantic beech, the useful elm, even the aspiring circuit of the lime, the regular round of the chestnut, and the almost moulded orange-tree, were

----

[1] It was not uncommon, after the circumadjacent country had been shut out, to endeavour to recover it by raising large mounts of earth to peep over the walls of the garden.

corrected by such fantastic admirers of symmetry. The compass and square were of more use in plantations than the nursery-man. The measured walk, the quincunx, and the etoile imposed their unsatisfying sameness on every royal and noble garden. Trees were headed, and their sides pared away; many French groves seem green chests set upon poles. Seats of marble, arbours, and summer-houses, terminated every vista; and symmetry, even where the space was too large to permit its being remarked at one view, was so essential, that, as Pope observed,

> . . . each alley has a brother,
> And half the garden just reflects the other.

Charles Bridgman

Bridgman, the next fashionable designer of gardens, was far more chaste; and whether from good sense, or that the nation had been struck and reformed by the admirable paper in the *Guardian* No. 173, he banished verdant sculpture, and did not even revert to the square precision of the foregoing age. He enlarged his plans, disdained to make every division tally to its opposite, and though he still adhered much to straight walks with high clipped hedges, they were only his great lines; the rest he diversified by wilderness, and with loose groves of oak, though still within surrounding hedges. I have observed in the garden at Gubbins in Hertfordshire many detached thoughts, that strongly indicate the dawn of modern taste. As his reformation gained footing, he ventured farther, and in the royal garden at Richmond dared to introduce cultivated fields, and even morsels of a forest appearance, by the sides of those endless and tiresome walks, that stretched out of one into another without intermission. But this was not till other innovators had broke loose too from rigid symmetry.

But the capital stroke, the leading step to all that has followed, was (I believe the first thought was Bridgman's) the destruction of walls for boundaries, and the invention of *fossés*—an attempt then deemed so astonishing, that the common people called them 'Ha! Ha's!' to express their surprise at finding a sudden and unperceived check to their walk.

One of the first gardens planted in this simple though still formal style, was my father's at Houghton. It was laid out by Mr Eyre, an imitator of Bridgman. It contains three-and-twenty acres, then reckoned a considerable portion.

I call a sunk fence the leading step, for these reasons. No sooner was this simple enchantment made, than levelling, mowing and rolling, followed. The contiguous ground of the park without the sunk fence was to be harmonized with the lawn within; and the garden in its turn was to be set free from its prim regularity, that it might assort with the wilder country without. The sunk fence ascertained the specific garden, but that it might not draw too obvious a line of distinction between the neat and the rude, the contiguous outlying parts came to be included in a kind of general design: and when Nature was taken into the plan, under improvements, every step that was made pointed out new beauties and inspired new ideas.

William Kent

At that moment appeared Kent, painter enough to taste the charms of landscape, bold and opinionative enough to dare and to dictate, and born with a genius to strike out a great system from the twilight of imperfect essays. He leaped the fence, and saw that all Nature was a garden. He felt the delicious contrast of hill and valley changing imperceptibly into each other, tasted the beauty of the gentle swell, or concave scoop, and remarked how loose groves crowned an easy eminence with happy ornament, and while they called in the distant view between their graceful stems, removed and extended the perspective by delusive comparison.

Thus the pencil of his imagination bestowed all the arts of landscape on the scenes he handled. The great principles on which he worked were perspective, and light and shade. Groups of trees broke too uniform or too extensive a lawn; evergreens and woods were opposed to the glare of the champain, and where the view was less fortunate, or so much exposed as to be beheld at once, he blotted out some parts by thick shades, to divide it into variety, or to make the richest scene more enchanting by reserving it to a farther advance of the spectator's steps. Thus, selecting favourite objects, and veiling deformities by screens of plantation, sometimes allowing the rudest waste to add its foil to the richest theatre, he realised the compositions of the greatest masters in painting. Where objects were wanting to animate his horizon, his taste as an architect could bestow immediate termination. His buildings, his seats, his temples, were more the works of his pencil than of his compasses. We owe the restoration of Greece and the diffusion of architecture to his skill in landscape.

But of all the beauties he added to the face of this beautiful country, none surpassed his management of water. Adieu to canals, circular basins, and cascades tumbling down marble steps, that last absurd magnificence of Italian and French villas. The forced elevation of cataracts was no more. The gentle stream was taught to serpentize seemingly at its pleasure, and where discontinued by different levels, its course appeared to be concealed by thickets properly interspersed, and glittered again at a distance where it might be supposed naturally to arrive. Its borders were smoothed, but preserved their waving irregularity. A few trees scattered here and there on its edges sprinkled the tame bank that accompanied its meanders; and when it disappeared among the hills, shades descending from the heights leaned towards its progress, and framed the distant point of light under which it was lost, as it turned aside to either hand of the blue horizon.

Thus dealing in none but the colours of Nature, and catching

L

its most favourable features, men saw a new creation opening
before their eyes. The living landscape was chastened or
polished, not transformed. Freedom was given to the forms of
trees; they extended their branches unrestricted, and where
any eminent oak, or master beech had escaped maiming and
survived the forest, bush and bramble was removed, and all its
honours were restored to distinguish and shade the plain.
Where the united plumage of an ancient wood extended wide
its undulating canopy, and stood venerable in its darkness,
Kent thinned the foremost ranks, and left but so many detached
and scattered trees, as softened the approach of gloom and
blended a chequered light with the thus lengthened shadows
of the remaining columns.

UVEDALE PRICE (1747–1829): from *An Essay on the Picturesque*
(1794)

The Picturesque Garden

Some French writer (I do not recollect who) ventures
to express a doubt, whether a tree waving in the wind with all
its branches free and untouched, may not possibly be an object
more worthy of admiration than one cut into form in the
gardens of Versailles. This bold sceptic in theory had most
probably his trees shorn like those of his sovereign.

It is equally probable that many an English gentleman has
felt deep regret when Mr Brown had improved some charming
trout stream into a piece of water; and that many a time afterwards, when walking on its naked banks, and disgusted with
its glare and formality, he has thought how beautifully fringed
those of his little brook once had been; how it sometimes ran
rapidly over the stones and shallows; and sometimes in a
narrower channel stole silently beneath the over-hanging
boughs. Many rich natural groups of trees he might remember

—now thinned and rounded into clumps; many sequestered and shady spots which he had loved when a boy—now all open and exposed, without shade or variety; and all these sacrifices made, not to his own, but to the taste of the day, and against his natural feelings.

It seems to me that there is something of patriotism in the praises Mr Walpole and Mr Mason have bestowed on English gardening; and that zeal for the honour of their country has made them, in the *general* view of the subject, overlook defects which they have themselves condemned. My love for my country is, I trust, not less ardent than theirs, but it has taken a different turn; and I feel anxious to free it from the disgrace of propagating a system, which, should it become universal, would disfigure the face of all Europe. I wish a more liberal and extended idea of improvement to prevail; that instead of the narrow, mechanical practice of a few English gardeners, the noble and varied works of the eminent painters of every age and of every country, and those of their supreme mistress, Nature, should be the great models of imitation.

If a taste for drawing and painting, and a knowledge of their principles, made a part of every gentleman's education; if, instead of hiring a professed improver to torture their grounds after an established model, each improved his own place according to general conceptions drawn from Nature and pictures, or suggested to him by his favourite masters in painting, or favourite parts of Nature—there might in time be a great variety in the styles of improvement, and all of them with peculiar excellencies. No two painters ever saw Nature with the same eyes; they tended to one point by a thousand different routes, and that makes the charm of an acquaintance with their various modes of conception and execution; but any of Mr Brown's followers might say, with great truth, 'We have but one idea among us.' (*From the Conclusion.*)

VII. *SOME CONTRIBUTIONS TO ÆSTHETIC THEORY*

LORD SHAFTESBURY (1671–1713): from *Characteristics* (1711)

Beauty dependent on Inward Perfection

Now if in the way of polite pleasure the study and love of beauty be essential, the study and love of symmetry and order, on which beauty depends, must also be essential in the same respect.

'Tis impossible we can advance the least in any relish or taste of outward symmetry and order, without acknowledging that the proportionate and regular state is the truly prosperous and natural in every subject. The same features which make deformity, create incommodiousness and disease. And the same shapes and proportions which make beauty, afford advantage by adapting to activity and use. Even in the imitative or designing arts . . . the truth or beauty of every figure or statue is measured from the perfection of Nature in her just adapting of every limb and proportion to the activity, strength, dexterity, life and vigour of the particular species or animal designed.

Thus beauty and truth are plainly joined with the notion of utility and convenience, even in the apprehension of every ingenious artist, the architect, the statuary, or the painter. 'Tis the same in the physician's way. Natural health is the just proportion, truth, and regular course of things in a constitution. 'Tis the inward beauty of the body. And when the harmony and just measures of the rising pulses, the circulating humours, and the moving airs or spirits, are disturbed or lost, deformity enters, and with it, calamity and ruin.

Should not this (one would imagine) be still the same case and hold equally as to the mind? Is there nothing there which tends to disturbance and dissolution? Is there no natural tenor, tone, or order of the passions or affections? No beauty or deformity in this moral kind? Or allowing that there really is, must it not, of consequence, in the same manner imply health or sickliness, prosperity or disaster? Will it not be found in this respect, above all, "that what is beautiful is harmonious and proportionable; what is harmonious and proportionable is true; and what is at once both beautiful and true is, of consequence, agreeable and good"?

Where then is this beauty or harmony to be found? How is this symmetry to be discovered and applied? Is it any other art than that of philosophy or the study of inward numbers and proportions which can exhibit this in life? If no other, who then can possibly have a taste of this kind, without being beholden to philosophy? Who can admire the outward beauties and not recur instantly to the inward, which are the most real and essential, and the most naturally affecting, and of the highest pleasure, as well as profit and advantage? (*Miscellany* III, Chapter ii.)

Moral Beauty the Highest Form of Beauty

However difficult or desperate it may appear in any artist to endeavour to bring perfection into his work, if he has not at least the idea of perfection to give him aim, he will be found very defective and mean in his performance. Though his intention be to please the world, he must nevertheless be, in a manner, above it, and fix his eye upon that consummate grace, that beauty of Nature, and that perfection of numbers which the rest of mankind, feeling only by the effect whilst ignorant of the cause, term the *je ne sçay quoy*, the unintelligible or the *I know not what*, and suppose to be a kind of charm or enchantment of which the artist himself can give no account. . . .

There can be no kind of writing which relates to men and manners where it is not necessary for the author to understand poetical and moral truth, the beauty of sentiments, the sublime of characters, and carry in his eye the model or exemplar of that natural grace which gives to every action its attractive charm. If he has naturally no eye or ear for these interior numbers, 'tis not likely he should be able to judge better of that exterior proportion and symmetry of composition which constitutes a legitimate piece.

Could we once convince ourselves of what is in itself so evident, "That in the very nature of things there must of necessity be the foundation of a right and wrong taste, as well in respect of inward characters and features as of outward person, behaviour, and action," we should be far more ashamed of ignorance and wrong judgment in the former than in the latter of these subjects. Even in the arts, which are mere imitations of that outward grace and beauty, we not only confess a taste, but make it a part of refined breeding to discover amidst the many false manners and ill styles the true and natural one, which represents the real beauty and Venus of the kind. 'Tis the like moral grace and Venus which, discovering itself in the turns of character and the variety of human affection, is copied by the writing artist. If he knows not this Venus, these graces, nor was ever struck with the beauty, the decorum of this inward kind, he can neither paint advantageously after the life nor in a feigned subject where he has full scope. For never can he, on these terms, represent merit and virtue, or mark deformity and blemish. Never can he with justice and true proportion assign the boundaries of either part, or separate the distant characters. The schemes must be defective and the draughts confused where the standard is weakly established and the measure out of use. Such a designer, who has so little feeling of these proportions, so little consciousness of this excellence or these perfections, will never be found able to describe a perfect character; or, what is more according to art, "express the effect and force of this perfection from the result of various and mixed characters of life."

And thus the sense of inward numbers, the knowledge and practice of the social virtues, and the familiarity and favour of the moral graces, are essential to the character of a deserving artist and just favourite of the Muses. Thus are the Arts and Virtues mutually friends; and thus the science of *virtuosi* and that of virtue itself become, in a manner, one and the same. (*Soliloquy, or Advice to an Author*, Part III, Section iii.)

FRANCIS HUTCHESON (1694–1746): from *An Inquiry into the Original of our Ideas of Beauty and Virtue* (1725)

The Perception of Beauty is to be distinguished from Sensation, Knowledge or Desire,

Let it be observed, that in the following papers, the word 'beauty' is taken for the idea raised in us, and 'a sense of beauty' for our power of receiving this idea. 'Harmony' also denotes our pleasant ideas arising from composition of sounds, and 'a good ear' (as it is generally taken) a power of perceiving this pleasure. In the following sections, an attempt is made to discover "what is the immediate occasion of these pleasant ideas, or what real quality in the objects ordinarily excites them."

It is of no consequence whether we call these ideas of beauty and harmony, perceptions of the external senses of seeing and hearing, or not. I should rather choose to call our power of perceiving these ideas, an *internal sense*, were it only for the convenience of distinguishing them from other sensations of seeing and hearing, which men may have without perception of beauty and harmony. It is plain from experience, that many men have, in the common meaning, the senses of seeing and hearing perfect enough, . . . and yet perhaps they shall find no pleasure in musical compositions, in painting architecture, natural landscape, or but a very weak one in comparison of what others enjoy from the same objects. This greater capacity of receiving such pleasant ideas we commonly call a *fine genius* or *taste*. In music we seem universally to acknowledge something like a distinct sense from the external one of hearing, and call it 'a good ear'; and the like distinction we should probably acknowledge in other objects, had we also got distinct names to denote these powers of perception by.

There will appear another reason perhaps hereafter, for calling this power of perceiving the ideas of *beauty* an *internal sense*, from this, that in some other affairs, where our external senses are not much concerned, we discern a sort of beauty, very like, in many respects, to that observed in sensible objects, and accompanied with like pleasure. Such is that beauty perceived in theorems, or universal truths, in general causes, and in some extensive principles of action.

Let every one here consider, how different we must suppose the perception to be, with which a poet is transported upon the prospect of any of those objects of natural beauty, which ravish us even in his description, from that cold, lifeless conception which we imagine in a dull critic, or one of the virtuosi, without what we call a *fine taste*. This latter class of men may have greater perfection in that knowledge which is derived from external sensation; they can tell all the specific differences of trees, herbs, minerals, metals; they know the form of every leaf, stalk, root, flower, and seed of all the species, about which the poet is often very ignorant; and yet the poet shall have a much more delightful perception of the whole; and not only the poet but any man of a fine taste. Our external senses may by measuring teach us all the proportions of architecture to the tenth of an inch, and the situation of every muscle in the human body; and a good memory may retain these: and yet there is still something farther necessary, not only to make a man a complete master in architecture, painting or statuary, but even a tolerable judge in these works; or

capable of receiving the highest pleasure in contemplating
them. Since then there are such different powers of perception,
where what are commonly called the external senses are the
same; since the most accurate knowledge of what the external
senses discover, often does not give the pleasure of beauty or
harmony, which yet one of a good taste will enjoy at once
without much knowledge; we may justly use another name for
these higher, and more delightful perceptions of beauty and
harmony, and call the power of receiving such impressions,
an internal sense. The difference of the perceptions seems
sufficient to vindicate the use of a different name, especially
when we are told in what meaning the word is applied.

This superior power of perception is justly called a sense,
because of its affinity to the other senses in this, that the
pleasure does not arise from any knowledge of principles,
proportions, causes, or of the usefulness of the object; but
strikes us at first with the idea of beauty: nor does the most
accurate knowledge increase this pleasure of beauty, however
it may superadd a distinct, rational pleasure from prospects of
advantage, or from the increase of knowledge.

And farther, the ideas of beauty and harmony, like other
sensible ideas, are necessarily pleasant to us, as well as
immediately so; neither can any resolution of our own, nor
any prospect of advantage or disadvantage, vary the beauty
or deformity of an object. For as in the external sensations,
no view of interest will make an object grateful, nor view
of detriment, distinct from immediate pain in the perception,
make it disagreeable to the sense; so propose the whole world
as a reward, or threaten the greatest evil, to make us approve
a deformed object, or disapprove a beautiful one, . . . our
sentiments of the forms, and our perceptions, would continue
invariably the same.

Hence it plainly appears, that some objects are immediately
the occasions of this pleasure of beauty, and that we have
senses fitted for perceiving it; and that it is distinct from that

joy which arises upon prospect of advantage. Nay, do we not often see convenience and use neglected to obtain beauty, without any other prospect of advantage in the beautiful form, than the suggesting the pleasant ideas of beauty? Now this shows us, that however we may pursue beautiful objects from self-love, with a view to obtain the pleasures of beauty, as in architecture, gardening and many other affairs; yet there must be a sense of beauty, antecedent to prospects even of this advantage, without which sense, these objects would not be thus advantageous, nor excite in us this pleasure which constitutes them advantageous. Our sense of beauty from objects, by which they are constituted good to us, is very distinct from our desire of them when they are thus constituted. Our desire of beauty may be counter-balanced by rewards or threatenings, but never our sense of it. . . .

Let it be observed, that by . . . beauty, is not understood any quality supposed to be in the object, which should of itself be beautiful, without relation to any mind which perceives it. For beauty, like other names of sensible ideas, properly denotes the perception of some mind; so cold, hot, sweet, bitter, denote the sensations in our minds, to which perhaps there is no resemblance in the objects, which excite these ideas in us, however we generally imagine otherwise. The ideas of beauty and harmony being excited upon our perception of some primary quality, and having relation to figure and time, may indeed have a nearer resemblance to objects, than these sensations, which seem not so much any pictures of objects, as modifications of the perceiving mind; and yet were there no mind with a sense of beauty to contemplate objects, I see not how they could be called beautiful. (Treatise I, Section I, ix–xvii.)

The Idea of Beauty is suggested by Forms which are characterized by Uniformity amidst Variety

The figures which excite in us the ideas of beauty, seem to be those in which there is uniformity amidst variety. There are many conceptions of objects which are agreeable upon other accounts, such as grandeur, novelty, sanctity, and some others. . . . But what we call beautiful in objects, to speak in the mathematical style, seems to be in a compound ratio of uniformity and variety: so that where the uniformity of bodies is equal, the beauty is as the variety; and where the variety is equal, the beauty is as the uniformity. . . . The same foundation we have for our sense of beauty in the works of Nature. In every part of the world which we call beautiful, there is a surprising uniformity amidst an almost infinite variety. . . .

As to the works of art, were we to run through the various artificial contrivances or structures, we should constantly find the foundation of the beauty which appears in them, to be some kind of uniformity, or unity of proportion among the parts, and of each part to the whole. As there is a greater diversity of proportions possible, and different kinds of uniformity, so there is room enough for that diversity of fancies observable in architecture, gardening, and such like arts in different nations; they all may have uniformity, though the parts in one may differ from those in another. The Chinese or Persian buildings are not like the Grecian and Roman, and yet the former have their uniformity of the various parts to each other, and to the whole, as well as the latter. In that kind of architecture which the Europeans call regular, the uniformity of parts is very obvious, the several parts are regular figures, and either equal or similar at least in the same range; . . . and though other countries do not follow the Grecian or Roman proportions, yet there is even among them a proportion retained, a uniformity, and resemblance of corresponding figures; and every deviation in one part from that proportion which is observed in the rest of the building, is displeasing to every eye, and destroys, or diminishes at least, the beauty of the whole.

The same might be observed through all other works of art, even to the meanest utensil; the beauty of every one of which we shall always find to have the same foundation of uniformity and variety, without which they appear mean, irregular and deformed. (Treatise I, Section II, iii–viii.)

Associations of Ideas may affect our Sense of Beauty, but the Sense of Beauty is antecedent to Custom, Habit, Education, Prospect of Advantage, or Association of Ideas

Nothing is more ordinary among those, who after Mr Locke have rejected *innate ideas*, than to allege that all our relish for beauty and order is either from prospect of advantage, custom, or education. . . .

The association of ideas above hinted at, is one great cause of the apparent diversity of fancies in the sense of beauty as well as in the external senses; and often makes men have an aversion to objects of beauty, and a liking to others void of it, but under different conceptions than those of beauty or deformity. . . .

In like manner it is known, that all the circumstances of actions, or places, or dresses of persons, or voice, or song, which have occurred at any time together, when we were strongly affected by any passion, will be so connected that any one of these will make all the rest recur. And this is often the occasion both of great pleasure and pain, delight and aversion to many objects, which of themselves might have been per-fectly indifferent to us; but these approbations, or distastes, are remote from the ideas of beauty, being plainly different ideas. . . . Had we no natural sense of beauty from uniformity, custom could never have made us imagine any beauty in objects; if we had had no ear, custom could never have given us the pleasures of harmony. When we have these natural senses antecedently, custom may make us capable of extending our views farther, and of receiving more complex ideas of beauty in bodies, or harmony in sounds, by increasing our attention and quickness of perception. But however custom may increase our power of receiving or comparing complex ideas, yet it seems rather to weaken than strengthen the ideas of beauty or the impressions of pleasure from regular objects; else how is it possible that any person could go into the open air on a sunny day, or clear evening, without the most extravagant raptures, such as Milton represents our ancestor in upon his first creation? For such any person would certainly fall into, upon the first representation of such a scene.

Custom in like manner may make it easier for any person to discern the use of a complex machine, and approve it as advantageous; but he would never have imagined it beautiful, had he no natural sense of beauty. Custom may make us quicker in apprehending the truth of complex theorems, but we all find the pleasure or beauty of theorems as strong at first as ever. Custom makes us more capable of retaining and comparing complex ideas, so as to discern more complicated uniformity, which escapes the observation of novices in any art; but all this presupposes a natural sense of beauty in uniformity: for had there been nothing in forms, which was constituted the necessary occasion of pleasure to our senses, no repetition of indifferent ideas as to pleasure or pain, beauty or deformity, could ever have made them grow pleasing or displeasing.

The effect of education is this, that thereby we receive many speculative opinions, which are sometimes true and sometimes false; and are often led to believe that objects may be naturally apt to give pleasure or pain to our external senses, which in reality have no such qualities. And farther, by education there are some strong associations of ideas without any reason, by mere accident sometimes, as well as by design, which it is very hard for us ever after to break asunder. Thus aversions are raised to darkness, and to many kinds of meat, and to certain innocent actions: approbations without ground are raised in like manner. But in all these instances, education never makes us apprehend any qualities in objects, which we have not *naturally* senses capable of perceiving. . . .

Thus education and custom may influence our internal senses, where they *are* antecedently, by enlarging the capacity of our minds to retain and compare the parts of complex compositions: and then if the finest objects are presented to us, we grow conscious of a pleasure far superior to what common performances excite. But all this presupposes our sense of beauty to be natural. (Treatise I, Section VI, viii: Section VII, iii.)

EDMUND BURKE (1729–97): from *A Philosophical Enquiry into the Origin of our Ideas of the Sublime and the Beautiful* (1756)

(*a*) *The Nature of Beauty*

The general application of this quality [beauty] to virtue has a strong tendency to confound our ideas of things; and it has given rise to an infinite deal of whimsical theory; as the affixing the name of beauty to proportion, congruity, and perfection, as well as to qualities of things yet more remote from our natural ideas of it, and from one another, has tended to confound our ideas of beauty, and left us no standard or rule to judge by, that was not even more uncertain and fallacious than our own fancies. This loose and inaccurate manner of speaking has therefore misled us both in the theory of taste and of morals; and induced us to remove the science of our duties from their proper basis (our reason, our relations, and our necessities) to rest it upon foundations altogether visionary and unsubstantial.

Having endeavoured to show what beauty is not, it remains that we should examine, at least with equal attention, in what it really consists. Beauty is a thing much too affecting not to depend upon some positive qualities. And, since it is no creature of our reason, since it strikes us without any reference to use, and even where no use at all can be discerned, since the order and method of nature is generally very different from our measures and proportions, we must conclude that beauty is, for the greater part, some quality in bodies acting mechanically upon the human mind by the intervention of the senses. We ought therefore to consider attentively in what manner those sensible qualities are disposed, in such things as by experience we find beautiful, or which excite in us the passion of love, or some correspondent affection.

．　　．　　．　　．　　．

On the whole, the qualities of beauty, as they are merely sensible qualities, are the following; First, to be comparatively small. Secondly, to be smooth. Thirdly, to have a variety in the direction of the parts; but, fourthly, to have those parts not angular, but melted as it were into each other. Fifthly, to be of a delicate frame, without any remarkable appearance of strength. Sixthly, to have its colours clear and bright, but not very strong and glaring. Seventhly, or if it should have any glaring colour, to have it diversified with others. These are, I believe, the properties on which beauty depends; properties that operate by nature, and are less liable to be altered by caprice, or confounded by a diversity of tastes, than any other. (Part III, Sections xi–xii, xviii.)

(b) The Nature of the Sublime

Whatever is fitted in any sort to excite the ideas of pain and danger, that is to say, whatever is in any sort terrible, or is conversant about terrible objects, or operates in a manner analogous to terror, is a source of the *sublime*; that is, it is productive of the strongest emotion which the mind is capable of feeling. I say the strongest emotion, because I am satisfied the ideas of pain are more powerful than those which enter on the part of pleasure. . . .

The passion caused by the great and sublime in *Nature*, when those causes operate most powerfully, is astonishment: and astonishment is that state of the soul, in which all its motions are suspended, with some degree of horror. In this case the mind is so entirely filled with its object, that it cannot entertain any other, nor by consequence reason on that object which employs it. Hence arises the great power of the sublime, that, far from being produced by them, it anticipates our reasonings, and hurries us on by an irresistible force. Astonishment, as I have said, is the effect of the sublime in its highest degree; the inferior effects are admiration, reverence, and respect.

No passion so effectually robs the mind of all its powers of acting and reasoning as *fear*. For fear being an apprehension of pain or death, it operates in a manner that resembles actual pain. Whatever therefore is terrible, with regard to sight, is sublime too, whether this cause of terror be endued with greatness of dimensions or not; for it is impossible to look on anything as trifling, or contemptible, that may be dangerous.

.   .   .   .   .

Besides those things which *directly* suggest the idea of danger, and those which produce a similar effect from a mechanical cause, I know of nothing sublime, which is not some modification of power. And this branch rises, as naturally as the other two branches, from terror, the common stock of everything that is sublime. The idea of power, at first view, seems of the class of those indifferent ones, which may equally belong to pain or to pleasure. But in reality, the affection, arising from the idea of vast power, is extremely remote from that neutral character. For first, we must remember, that the idea of pain, in its highest degree, is much stronger than the highest degree of pleasure; and that it preserves the same superiority through all the subordinate gradations. From hence it is, that where the chances for equal degrees of suffering or enjoyment are in any sort equal, the idea of the suffering must always be prevalent. And indeed the ideas of pain, and, above all, of death, are so very affecting, that whilst we remain in the presence of whatever is supposed to have the power of inflicting either, it is impossible to be perfectly free from terror. Again, we know by experience, that, for the enjoyment of pleasure, no great efforts of power are at all necessary; nay, we know, that such efforts would go a great way towards destroying our satisfaction: for pleasure must be stolen, and not forced upon us; pleasure follows the will; and therefore we are generally affected with it by many things of a force greatly inferior to our own. But pain is always inflicted by a power in some way superior, because we never submit to pain willingly. So that strength, violence, pain and terror, are ideas that rush in upon the mind together. Look at a man, or any other animal of prodigious strength, and what is your idea before reflection? Is it that this strength will be subservient to you, to your ease, to your pleasure, to your interest in any sense? No; the emotion you feel is, lest this enormous strength should be employed to the purposes of rapine and destruction. That power derives all its sublimity from the terror with which it is generally accompanied, will appear evident from its effect in the very few cases, in which it may be possible to strip a considerable degree of strength of its ability to hurt. When you do this, you spoil it of everything sublime, and it immediately becomes contemptible. An ox is a creature of vast strength; but he is an innocent creature, extremely serviceable, and not at all dangerous; for which reason the idea of an ox is by no means grand. A bull is strong too: but his strength is of another kind; often very destructive, seldom (at least amongst us) of any use in our business; the idea of a bull is therefore great, and it has

M

frequently a place in sublime descriptions and elevating comparisons. Let us look at another strong animal, in the two distinct lights in which we may consider him. The horse in the light of a useful beast, fit for the plough, the road, the draft; in every social useful light, the horse has nothing sublime: but is it thus that we are affected with him, "whose neck is clothed with thunder, the glory of whose nostrils is terrible, who swalloweth the ground with fierceness and rage, neither believeth that it is the sound of the trumpet"? In this description, the useful character of the horse entirely disappears, and the terrible and the sublime blaze out together.

.   .   .   .   .

Greatness of dimension is a powerful cause of the sublime. This is too evident, and the observation too common, to need any illustration: it is not so common to consider in what ways greatness of dimension, vastness of extent or quantity, has the most striking effect. For, certainly, there are ways, and modes, wherein the same quantity of extension shall produce greater effects than it is found to do in others. Extension is either in length, height, or depth. Of these the length strikes least; an hundred yards of even ground will never work such an effect as a tower an hundred yards high, or a rock or mountain of that altitude. I am apt to imagine likewise, that height is less grand than depth; and that we are more struck at looking down from a precipice, than looking up at an object of equal height; but of that I am not very positive. A perpendicular has more force in forming the sublime, than an inclined plane; and the effects of a rugged and broken surface seem stronger than where it is smooth and polished. It would carry us out of our way to enter in this place into the cause of these appearances; but certain it is they afford a large and fruitful field of speculation. However, it may not be amiss to add to these remarks upon magnitude, that, as the great extreme of dimension is sublime, so the last extreme of littleness is in some measure sublime likewise: when we attend to the infinite divisibility of matter, when we pursue animal life into these excessively small, and yet organized beings, that escape the nicest inquisition of the sense; when we push our discoveries yet downward, and consider those creatures so many degrees yet smaller, and the still diminishing scale of existence, in tracing which the imagination is lost as well as the sense; we become amazed and confounded at the wonders of minuteness; nor can we distinguish in its effect this extreme of littleness from the vast itself. For division must be infinite as well as addition; because the idea of a perfect unity can no more be arrived at, than that of a complete whole, to which nothing may be added.

Another source of the sublime is *Infinity*; if it does not rather belong to the last. Infinity has a tendency to fill the mind with that sort of delightful horror, which is the most genuine effect, and truest test of the sublime. There are scarce any things which can become the objects of our senses, that are really and in their own nature infinite. But the eye not being able to perceive the bounds of many things, they seem to be infinite, and they produce the same effects as if they were really so. We are deceived in the like manner, if the parts of some large object are so continued to any indefinite number, that the imagination meets no check which may hinder its extending them at pleasure. (Part I, Section vii; Part II, Sections i, ii, v, vii, viii.)

(c) *The Sublime and Beautiful compared*

On closing this general view of Beauty, it naturally occurs, that we should compare it with the Sublime; and in this comparison there appears a remarkable contrast. For sublime objects are vast in their dimensions, beautiful ones comparatively small: beauty should be smooth and polished; the great, rugged and negligent; beauty should shun the right line, yet deviate from it insensibly; the great in many cases loves the right line; and when it deviates, it often makes a strong deviation: beauty should not be obscure; the great ought to be dark and gloomy: beauty should be light and delicate; the great ought to be solid, and even massive. They are indeed ideas of a very different nature, one being founded on pain, the other on pleasure; and however they may vary afterwards from the direct nature of their causes, yet these causes keep up an eternal distinction between them, a distinction never to be forgotten by any whose business it is to affect the passions. In the infinite variety of natural combinations, we must expect to find the qualities of things, the most remote imaginable from each other, united in the same object. We must expect also to find combinations of the same kind in the works of art. But when we consider the power of an object upon our passions, we must know that when anything is intended to affect the mind by the force of some predominant property, the affection produced is like to be the more uniform and perfect, if all the other properties or qualities of the object be of the same nature, and tending to the same design as the principal. (Part III, Section xxvii.)

ARCHIBALD ALISON (1757–1839): from *On Taste* (1790)

Beauty as Expression: the Force of Association of Ideas

The illustrations that have been offered in the course of this essay upon the origin of the sublimity and beauty of some of the principal qualities of matter, seem to afford sufficient evidence for the following conclusions:

I. That each of these qualities is either from Nature, from experience, or from accident, the sign of some quality capable of producing emotion, or the exercise of some moral affection. And,

II. That when these associations are dissolved, or in other words, when the material qualities cease to be significant of the associated qualities, they cease also to produce the emotions, either of sublimity or beauty.

If these conclusions are admitted, it appears necessarily to follow, that the beauty and sublimity of such objects is to be ascribed not to the material qualities themselves, but to the qualities they signify; and, of consequence, that the qualities of matter are not to be considered as sublime or beautiful in themselves, but as being the *signs* or *expressions* of such qualities, as, by the constitution of our nature, are fitted to produce pleasing or interesting emotion. . . .

The qualities of mind which are capable of producing emotion, are either its active or its passive qualities; either its *powers* and capacities, as beneficence, wisdom, fortitude, invention, fancy, etc., or its *feelings and affections*, as love, joy, hope, gratitude, purity, fidelity, innocence, etc. . . .

As it is only, however, through the medium of matter, that, in the present condition of our being, the qualities of mind are known to us, the qualities of matter become necessarily expressive to us of all the qualities of mind they signify. They may be the signs, therefore, or expressions of these mental qualities, in the following ways: I. As the immediate signs of the powers or capacities of mind. It is thus, that all the works of human art or design, are directly significant to us of the wisdom, the invention, the taste, or the benevolence of the artist; and the works of Nature, of the power, the wisdom, and the beneficence of the Divine artist. II. As the signs of all those affections, or dispositions of mind, which we love, or with which we are formed to sympathize. It is thus that the notes and motions of animals are expressive to us of their happiness and joy; that the tones of the human voice are significant of the various emotions by which it is animated; and that all the affections which we either love or admire in the human mind, are directly signified to us by the various appearances of the countenance and form.

These may be called the *direct* expressions of mind; and the material qualities which signify such powers or affections, produce in us immediately the peculiar emotions which, by the laws of our nature, the mental qualities are fitted to produce. But beside these, there are other means by which the qualities of matter may be significant to us of the qualities of mind, *indirectly*, or by means of less universal and less permanent relations.

1. From experience, when peculiar forms or appearances of matter are considered as the *means* or *instruments* by which those feelings or affections of mind are produced with which we sympathise, or in which we are interested. It is thus that the productions of art are in so many various ways significant to us of the conveniences, the pleasures, or the happiness they bestow upon human life, and as the *signs* of happiness affect us with the emotion this happiness itself is destined to produce. It is thus also, that the scenes of Nature acquire such an accession of beauty, when we consider them as fitted, with such exquisite wisdom, for the habitation of so many classes of sentient being: and when they become thus expressive to us of all the varied happiness they produce, and contain, and conceal.

2. From analogy or resemblance; from that resemblance which has everywhere been felt between the qualities of matter and of mind, and by which the former becomes so powerfully expressive to us of the latter. It is thus, that the colours, the sounds, the forms, and above all, perhaps, the motions of inanimate objects, are so universally felt as resembling peculiar qualities or affections of mind, and when thus felt, are so productive of the analogous emotion; that the personification of matter is so strongly marked in every period of the history

of human thought; and that the poet, while he gives life and animation to everything around him, is not displaying his own invention, but only obeying one of the most powerful laws which regulate the imagination of man.

3. From association (in the proper sense of that term), when by means of education, of fortune, or of accident, material objects are connected with pleasing or interesting qualities of mind; and from this connection become forever afterwards expressive of them. It is thus that colours, forms, etc., derive their temporary beauty from fashion; that the objects which have been devoted to religion, to patriotism or to honour, affect us with all the emotions of the qualities of which they become significant; that the beauty of natural scenery is so often exalted by the record of the events it has witnessed; and that in every country, the scenes which have the deepest effect upon the admiration of the people, are those which have become sacred by the memory of ancient virtue, or ancient glory.

4. From *individual* association; when certain qualities or appearances of matter, are connected with our own private affections or remembrances; and when they give to these material qualities or appearances a character of interest which is solely the result of our own memory and affections.

Of the reality of these expressions I believe no person can doubt: and whoever will attend to the power and extent of their influence, will, I think, soon be persuaded, that they are sufficient to account for all the beauty or sublimity we discover in the qualities of matter. (Essay II, Chapter VI, Section vi.)

WILLIAM GILPIN (1724–1804): from *Three Essays: on Picturesque Beauty, on Picturesque Travel, and on Sketching Landscape* (1792)

The Nature of Picturesque Beauty

Disputes about beauty might perhaps be involved in less confusion, if a distinction were established, which certainly exists, between such objects as are beautiful, and such as are picturesque—between those which please the eye in their natural state, and those which please from some quality capable of being illustrated in painting. . . .

How far Mr Burke may be right in making smoothness the most considerable source of beauty, I rather doubt. A considerable one it certainly is. . . . But in picturesque representation it seems somewhat odd, yet we shall perhaps find it equally true, that the reverse of this is the case; and that the ideas of neat and smooth, instead of being picturesque, in fact disqualify the object, in which they reside, from any pretensions to picturesque beauty. Nay, farther, we do not scruple to assert, that roughness forms the most essential point of difference between the beautiful and the picturesque; as it seems to be that particular quality which makes objects chiefly pleasing in painting. I use the general term roughness; but properly speaking roughness relates only to the surfaces of bodies: when we speak of their delineation, we use the word *ruggedness*. Both ideas, however, equally enter into the picturesque; and both are observable in the smaller, as well as in the larger parts of Nature—in the outline and bark of a tree, as in the rude summit and craggy sides of a mountain. . . .

A piece of Palladian architecture may be elegant in the last degree. The proportion of its parts, the propriety of its ornaments, and the symmetry of the whole, may be highly pleasing. But if we introduce it in a picture, it immediately becomes a formal object, and ceases to please. Should we wish to give it picturesque beauty, we must use the mallet, instead of the chisel: we must beat down one half of it, deface the other, and throw the mutilated members around in heaps. In short, from a smooth building we must turn it into a rough ruin. No painter, who had the choice of the two objects, would hesitate a moment.

Again, why does an elegant piece of garden-ground make no figure on canvas? The shape is pleasing; the combination of the objects harmonious; and the winding of the walk in the very line of beauty. All this is true; but the smoothness of the whole, though right, and as it should be in Nature, offends in picture. Turn the lawn into a piece of broken ground, plant rugged oaks instead of flowering shrubs, break the edges of the walk, give it the rudeness of a road, mark it with wheel-tracks, and scatter around a few stones, and brushwood; in a word, instead of making the whole smooth, make it rough; and you make it also picturesque. All the other ingredients of beauty it already possessed. (From *Essay I, On Picturesque Beauty*.)

UVEDALE PRICE (1747–1829): from *An Essay on the Picturesque, as compared with the Sublime and Beautiful; and, on the Use of studying Pictures, for the purpose of improving real Landscape* (1794)

The principles of those two leading characters in Nature, the sublime and the beautiful, have been fully illustrated and discriminated by a great master; but even when I first read that most original work, I felt that there were numberless objects which give great delight to the eye, and yet differ as widely from the beautiful as from the sublime. The reflections I have since been led to make have convinced me that these objects form a distinct class, and belong to what may properly be called the picturesque.

That term (as we may judge from its etymology) is applied

only to objects of sight, and that indeed in so confined a manner as to be supposed merely to have a reference to the art from which it is named. I am well convinced, however, that the name and reference only are limited and uncertain, and that the qualities which make objects picturesque are not only as distinct as those which make them beautiful or sublime, but are equally extended to all our sensations, by whatever organs they are received; and that music (though it appears like a solecism) may be as truly picturesque, according to the general principles of picturesqueness, as it may be beautiful or sublime, according to those of beauty or sublimity. . . .

I must here observe (and I wish the reader to keep it in his mind) that the enquiry is not in what sense certain words are used in the best authors, still less what is their common and vulgar use and abuse; but whether there are certain qualities which uniformly produce the same effects in all visible objects, and, according to the same analogy, in objects of hearing and of all the other senses; and which qualities (though frequently blended and united with others in the same object or set of objects) may be separated from them, and assigned to the class to which they belong.

If it can be shown that a character composed of these qualities, and distinct from all others, does prevail through all Nature; if it can be traced in the different objects of art and of Nature, and appears consistent throughout, it surely deserves a distinct title; but with respect to the real ground of enquiry, it matters little whether such a character, or the set of objects belonging to it, is called beautiful, sublime, or picturesque, or by any other name, or by no name at all. . . .

According to Mr Burke, one of the most essential qualities of beauty is smoothness; now, as the perfection of smoothness is absolute equality and uniformity of surface, wherever that prevails there can be but little variety or intricacy; as, for instance, in smooth level banks on a small, or in naked downs on a large scale. Another essential quality of beauty is gradual variation; that is (to make use of Mr Burke's expression) where the lines do not vary in a sudden and broken manner, and where there is no sudden protuberance. It requires but little reflection to perceive, that the exclusion of all but flowing lines cannot promote variety; and that sudden protuberances, and lines that cross each other in a sudden and broken manner, are among the most fruitful causes of intricacy.

I am therefore persuaded, that the two opposite qualities of roughness, and of sudden variation, joined to that of irregularity, are the most efficient causes of the picturesque.

This, I think, will appear very clearly, if we take a view of those objects, both natural and artificial, that are allowed to be picturesque, and compare them with those which are as generally allowed to be beautiful.

A temple or palace of Grecian architecture in its perfect entire state, and its surface and colour smooth and even, either in painting or reality, is beautiful; in ruin it is picturesque. . . .

Gothic architecture is generally considered as more picturesque, though less beautiful, than Grecian; and, upon the same principle that a ruin is more so than a new edifice. The first thing that strikes the eye in approaching any building is the general outline against the sky (or whatever it may be opposed to) and the effect of the openings: in Grecian buildings the general lines of the roof are straight, and even when varied and adorned by a dome or a pediment, the whole has a character of symmetry and regularity.

In Gothic buildings, the outline of the summit presents such a variety of forms, of turrets and pinnacles, some open, some fretted and variously enriched, that even where there is an exact correspondence of parts, it is often disguised by an appearance of splendid confusion and irregularity. In the doors and windows of Gothic churches, the pointed arch has as much variety as any regular figure can well have, the eye too is not so strongly conducted from the top of the one to that of the other, as by the parallel lines of the Grecian; and every person must be struck with the extreme richness and intricacy of some of the principal windows of our cathedrals and ruined abbeys. In these last is displayed the triumph of the picturesque; and its charms to a painter's eye are often so great as to rival those of beauty itself. . . .

Among painters, Salvator Rosa is one of the most remarkable for his picturesque style, and in no other master are seen such abrupt and rugged forms, such sudden deviations both in his figures and his landscapes; and the roughness and broken touches of his pencilling admirably accord with the objects they characterise.

Guido, on the other hand, was as eminent for beauty; in his celestial countenances are the happiest examples of gradual variation—of lines that melt and flow into each other; no sudden break—nothing that can disturb that pleasing languor which the union of all that constitutes beauty impresses on the soul. . . . But the works even of this great master show us how unavoidably an attention to mere beauty and flow of outline will lead towards sameness and insipidity. If this has happened to a painter of such high excellence, . . . what must be the case with men who have been tethered all their lives in a clump or a belt? . . . (Chapter III.)

These are the principal circumstances by which the picturesque is separated from the beautiful. It is equally distinct from the sublime; for though there are some qualities common to them both, yet they differ in many essential points, and proceed from very different causes. In the first place, greatness of dimension is a powerful cause of the sublime; the picturesque has no connection with dimension of any kind (in which it differs from the beautiful also) and is as often found in the smallest as in the largest objects. The sublime, being founded on principles of awe and terror, never descends to anything light or playful; the picturesque, whose characteristics are intricacy and variety, is equally adapted to the grandest and to the gayest scenery. Infinity is one of the most efficient causes of the sublime; the boundless ocean, for that reason, inspires awful sensations: to give it picturesqueness you must destroy that cause of its sublimity; for it is on the shape and disposition of its boundaries that the picturesque in great measure must depend. . . .

I think we may conclude, that where an object, or a set of objects, is without smoothness or grandeur, but from its intricacy, its sudden and irregular deviations, its variety of forms, tints, and lights and shadows, is interesting to a cultivated eye, it is simply picturesque. Such, for instance, are the rough banks that often inclose a bye-road or a hollow lane. Imagine the size of these banks and the space between them to be increased till the lane becomes a deep dell, the coves large caverns, the peeping stones hanging rocks, so that the whole may impress an idea of awe and grandeur; the sublime will then be mixed with the picturesque, though the scale only, not the style of the scenery, would be changed. On the other hand, if parts of the banks were smooth and gently sloping, or the middle space a soft close-bitten turf, or if a gentle stream passed between them, whose clear unbroken surface reflected all their varieties, the beautiful and the picturesque, by means of that softness and smoothness, would then be united. (Chapter IV.)

The effects of the picturesque, when mixed with the sublime or the beautiful, have been already considered. It will be found as frequently mixed with ugliness, and its effects when so mixed to be perfectly consistent with all that has been mentioned of its effects and qualities. Ugliness, like beauty, in itself is not picturesque, for it has, simply considered, no strongly marked features; but when the last-mentioned character is added either to beauty or to ugliness, they become more striking and varied, and whatever may be the sensations they excite, they always, by means of that addition, more strongly attract the attention. We are amused and occupied by ugly objects if they are also picturesque, just as we are by a rough, and in other respects a disagreeable mind, provided it has a marked and peculiar character; without it, mere outward ugliness, or mere inward rudeness, are simply disagreeable. (Chapter IX.)

NOTES

Frontispiece. The frontispiece shows the south front of Stowe House, seen across the lake and park from one of Kent's Doric lodges. Stowe, which is now the home of a public school, originally became famous as the seat of the first Lord Cobham, who began to develop the estate in 1713. It was a great centre of Whig society through most of the eighteenth century, and in its conception and design mirrored much of the political thought and artistic outlook of the age. Vanbrugh, Kent, Leoni, Gibbs, and Robert Adam all contributed to the architecture of the house, or of other buildings in the park. Vanbrugh and Bridgeman were responsible for the original semi-formal layout of the gardens, but these were afterwards transformed under 'Capability' Brown, to bring them into line with the later conception of the 'landscape garden.'

Introduction

p. 12. *Earl of Burlington.* Burlington was the patron of William Kent and encouraged the productions of Colin Campbell (? – 1729), the architect of Houghton Hall, Norfolk, and Giacomo Leoni (1686–1746), the designer of Moor Park, Hertfordshire. It is hardly too much to say that the Palladian movement in eighteenth-century English architecture was mainly inspired by him. With his name may be associated those of other patrons, such as the Earl of Pembroke, Sir Robert Walpole, the Dukes of Bedford and Northumberland, and Christopher Codrington.

p. 15. *Romanticism.* This intermingling of elements in the taste of the time is well illustrated in E. F. Carritt's *Calendar of British Taste,* 1600–1800 (Routledge, 1949). See Introduction, p. ix, and text passim.

p. 20. *Longinus.* Greek philosopher and grammarian of the third century A.D. Modern scholarship tends to reject the ascription of the treatise to him and to place the date of its composition in the first rather than the third century. See Introduction to *Longinus on the Sublime,* edited by Rhys Roberts (second edition: Cambridge, 1907).

p. 23. *The Fairy Way of Writing.* Addison owed the phrase to Dryden, who, in his "Epistle Dedicatory" to *King Arthur* (1691), writes of "the fairy kind of writing which depends only upon the force of the imagination."

p. 25. *Tom Jones.* See especially Book IX, chapter i, and compare Fielding's preface to *Joseph Andrews.* The novel was already far removed from Johnson's definition: "a smooth tale, mostly of love."

p. 26. *The Wartons and Milton.* It is noteworthy that Thomas Warton's *Observations on "The Faerie Queene"* (1754) contained numerous references to Milton.
Milton's view of poetry. Implied in his major poems—*e.g.*, *Paradise Lost*, vii. 1–39, and discussed briefly in *Reason of Church Government.*

p. 29. *English landscape painting.* See Horace Walpole, *Anecdotes of Painting,* edited by Wornum, ii, 333. The effects of this vogue of landscape painting were clearly seen in English poetry from about 1730. The parts of Thomson's *Seasons* written after his grand tour with Charles Talbot in 1730–31 show a greatly increased sense of the pictorial effects of landscape, and this heightened interest was doubtless due as much as Thomson's study of painting as to his observation of natural scenery. A well-known stanza of *The Castle of Indolence* reflects the common view of the great seventeenth-century landscape masters:

> Sometimes the pencil, in cool airy halls,
> Bade the gay bloom of vernal landskips rise,
> Or Autumn's varied shades imbrown the walls:
> Now the black tempest strikes the astonished eyes;
> Now down the steep the flashing torrent flies;
> The trembling sun now plys o'er ocean blue,
> And now rude mountains frown amid the skies;
> Whate'er Lorrain light touched with softening hue,
> Or savage Rosa dashed, or learnèd Poussin drew.

p. 30. *The natural garden.* The conception of the natural garden was partly inspired by the descriptions of ideal natural scenes to be found in Milton and in Greek pastoral poetry. The influence of pastoral landscape painters such as Claude and Poussin was equally important.
Lancelot "Capability" Brown (1715–83). One of the best-known landscape gardeners of the period. He was so styled because, when called in to advise on the laying out of an estate, he would commonly refer to the "great capability of improvement" he

saw there. Brown was head gardener at Stowe from 1740 to 1750 and then set up as a professional improver. See Dorothy Stroud, *Capability Brown* (London, 1951).

p. 31. *The classical school of architecture.* Other great architects of this same school were Colin Campbell (died 1734), the author of *Vitruvius Britannicus*, who was responsible for Houghton Hall, in Norfolk, James Gibbs (1682–1754), the architect of St Martin-in-the-Fields, Isaac Ware (died 1766), who built Chesterfield House and other London houses, and Sir William Chambers (1726–96), the architect of Somerset House, London, with its nicely balanced and impressive frontage overlooking the river. To this same tradition belonged the work of the Woods, in Bath, of John Carr, in York, and of Sir James Gandon, in Dublin.

Satire on baroque buildings. For example, Pope's epigram on Blenheim:

> 'Tis very fine,
> But where d'ye sleep, or where d'ye dine?
> I find, by all you have been telling
> That 'tis a house, but not a dwelling.

p. 32. *Revival of Gothic.* The interest taken in medieval Gothic architecture was a much more powerful influence in early Romantic literature in England than the study of medieval literature.

p. 47. *Bath.* Even in 1766 Horace Walpole spoke very slightingly of Bath and Bristol.

Ossian. It is noteworthy that Blair's critical dissertation (1763) on *Ossian*, although conservative in method, laid special stress on the natural sublimity depicted by this poet:

> The scenery throughout is wild and romantic. The extended heath by the sea-shore; the mountain shrouded with mist; the torrent rushing through a solitary valley; the scattered oaks, and the tombs of warriors overgrown with moss; all produce a solemn attention in the mind.

p. 51. *Achievement of the period in literary and æsthetic criticism.* Whereas in the previous two centuries English criticism had owed much to Continental writers, in the eighteenth century the situation was reversed; and French and German critics and philosophers were greatly influenced by the critical and æsthetic work of Addison and Shaftesbury, Hume, Hogarth, Burke, and Lord Kames. Kant's first published essay, his *Observations on the Sentiments of the Beautiful and the Sublime* (1764), Lessing's *Laocoön* (1766), and Kant's *Critique of Judgment* (1790) all contain significant echoes of their British forerunners.

N

Alexander Pope: from "An Essay on Criticism"

p. 53. This passage is an expression in memorable form of some of the leading articles of neo-classical poetic and critical faith. The views put forward are those of the age rather than of Pope as an individual. A later paragraph of the *Essay*, on the spirit of true criticism (ll. 233–262), is written in a much more liberal vein, and Pope's critical prefaces (see below) are much more modern and Romantic in spirit. In the present passage, however, we have the strict and illogical neo-classic doctrine: truth to Nature, and therefore artistic value, is to be attained through a study of the classics and the Rules deduced from them. The study of classical models and the exercise of reason are essential checks on the lawlessness of poetic fancy.

Nature, Wit, Judgment. See notes on pp. 223–225.

p. 54. *Mantuan muse, Maro.* Virgil (Publius, Vergilius Maro) was born in 70 B.C. near Mantua, in North Italy.

Stagyrite. Aristotle, a native of Stagira in Macedonia.

Lord Shaftesbury: from "Characteristics"

p. 55. The third Earl of Shaftesbury, grandson of the famous politician of Charles II's reign, was prevented by delicate health from taking an active part in politics, and devoted most of his short life to literature, art, and philosophy. His education was superintended by Locke, but he revolted against Locke's philosophy, and came chiefly under the influence of Plato and the English Platonists. His *Moralists* was an attempt to imitate Plato's *Dialogues*.

Shaftesbury was, however, of an original turn of mind, and dealt with moral, religious, and æsthetic topics in new ways. He made a deep impression on the thought of his time, and had considerable influence abroad as well as in Britain. Diderot and Leibnitz both acknowledged their debt to him, and his *Judgment of Hercules* anticipated to some extent the *Laocoön* of Lessing. His writings, of which the best known were *Moralists, a philosophical Rhapsody* (1709) and *Soliloquy, or Advice to an Author* (1710), were collected under the title *Characteristics of Men, Manners, Opinions and Times* (1711; enlarged 1713).

The passage given here deals with the acquirement of taste in the arts, and assumes without argument that the classics are the proper models for study.

Raphael, Carraccio. Raphael Sanzio (1483–1520) worked chiefly in

Rome after 1508. Lodovico Carraccio was born in Bologna in 1555 and founded an academy of painting there, in company with his nephews Agostino and Annibale. The work of this family was largely imitative of the effects of the great Renaissance masters, Raphael, Michelangelo, and Titian; but the Carracci were technically skilful, and the second flowering during the Renaissance of the Italian genius in painting owed much to them. The early eighteenth century had neither realized the superiority of Michelangelo nor distinguished between the merits of Raphael and L. Carraccio, who were frequently coupled at this time as the two great painters of the fifteenth century.

pp. 55, 56. *Japan work, Flemish style.* As a classicist and an aristocrat, Shaftesbury viewed with distrust both the contemporary enthusiasm for Oriental art and the popularity of the democratic painting of Flanders and Holland. Gildon adopted a similar attitude. The contrast drawn here between the painting of the Italian and of the Dutch and Flemish schools was followed by Reynolds and further developed by Ruskin.

Joseph Addison: from "The Spectator"

p. 56. *Bouhours.* Le père Bouhours (1628–1702), Jesuit philologist and literary critic, and author of *La manière de bien penser dans les ouvrages d'esprit* (1687).

Boileau. Nicolas Boileau-Despréaux (1636–1711) expresses this thought in the well-known sentence "Rien n'est beau que le vrai," in his Ninth Epistle.

Wit. Used in the sense of 'extravagance' or 'conceit.'

Goths. That is, characterized by barbarism or bad taste. This eighteenth-century use of the word has reference to the Goths' destruction of Roman civilization. Dryden, in his *Parallel of Poetry and Painting*, spoke of the need to avoid the "Gothic manner" and "barbarous ornaments," and referred to English tragi-comedy as "Gothic."

Charles Gildon: from "A Complete Art of Poetry"

p. 57. Charles Gildon (1665–1724) was a hack playwright and miscellaneous writer. Like many of his contemporaries, he fell foul of Pope, who attacked him in the *Epistle to Arbuthnot* and in *The Dunciad.* The *Complete Art of Poetry* is a clear statement of neoclassical critical doctrine. Gildon argues that the Rules are based on reason, and illustrated in the classics, and that their authority is not arbitrary, but derived from the artistic pleasure which all men find in classical works. As a rationalist, Gildon is naturally opposed to the idea of the liberty of genius, which was beginning to find support in his day.

Rules of art. Rules of the kind quoted, as deduced from the ancient Greek statues, were given by Du Piles in his note on line 145 of Du Fresnoy's *De Arte graphica.*

Gusto. The word is used, as in Shaftesbury, in the sense of 'keen æsthetic appreciation' or 'taste.'

Grotesque. The term was originally used of the painting or carving of foliage or animal forms such as seemed appropriate to grottoes, but by 1650 the word had come to mean 'distorted,' 'fantastic,' or 'exaggerated.'

Gothic. See note on "Goths" above, p. 195.

Japan Pictures. See note on "Japan work" above, p. 195.

Audrands, Simoneans, Edlinahs. Gérard Audran (1640–1703) was an engraver of Lyons, noted especially for his engravings of the paintings of Le Brun. His nephew Jean (1667–1756) engraved many of the works of Poussin. Gérard Edelinah (1640–1707) was another famous French engraver, and the same art was practised by his brothers Jean and Gaspard and by his son Nicolas. Simone Cantarini or Simone da Pesaro (1612–48) was an Italian painter and etcher and a disciple of Guido Reni.

Operas. Compare Addison's criticisms of this form, and especially of the Italian opera, in *The Spectator,* Nos. 5, 18, etc.

p. 58. *Alexander, Cæsar.* The comparison of Alexander the Great with Cæsar is an obvious one, but was doubtless made more popular by Plutarch's parallel Lives of these notable figures.

Shakespeare's monstrous irregularities. Ben Jonson refers to a similar line of argument in his *Timber* or *Discourses,* when he says that the players praised Shakespeare because he "never blotted a line."

p. 59. *Rules of Nature . . . liberty of mankind.* The paragraph echoes Pope's *Essay,* ll. 89–92.

p. 60. *Laws of Nature . . . a perpetuate existence.* Note that according to this classical absolutism the laws or rules of art are imagined as having a permanence not possessed by any other human institutions.

John Dennis: from "The Advancement and Reformation of Modern Poetry"

p. 61. John Dennis, who is not to be judged by the measure of Pope's animosity towards him, was, next to Dryden, the author of the most comprehensive body of criticism in English before the time of Addison, and one who had more insight than most of his contemporaries into the new trends in the literature of his time. His criticism is not entirely consistent, and perhaps he tended to become less liberal in outlook as he grew older; but he had the positive merit of seeing the inadequacy of the Rules and of servile imitation of the Classics, and he realized the essential place which passion or enthusiasm should have in the making of poetry and in the appreciation of it. Sublimity of feeling and expression was for him of higher value than purely formal beauty, and this is the main theme of his *Advancement and Reformation of Modern Poetry* and of his *Grounds of Criticism.*

Dennis's chief weakness as a theorist is that he is too much of a rationalist. This emphasis on reason—not unnatural in the age of Locke—leads him to over-emphasize the need for consistency and regularity in art, and to insist excessively on poetry's didactic function. From these premises spring his love of poetic justice and his criticism of the mixing of tragic and comic elements in drama. But these limitations do not obscure the value of his discussion of the place of passion in poetry. What chiefly detracts from the usefulness of his critical writing is his laborious and repetitive style.

Poetry without numbers. The idea that poetry does not consist in the use of verse, and that verse is not necessarily poetry, goes back to Aristotle's *Poetics,* i. 6–9. Renaissance critics took up the discussion again—*e.g.,* Sidney, in his *Apologie for Poetrie.*

p. 63. *A philosopher.* Dennis is probably hitting at Shaftesbury.

Isaac Watts: from the preface to "Horæ Lyricæ"

p. 65. A few of Watts's hymns are still in common use, but perhaps he is too little remembered as a minor poet of his age. His *Horæ Lyricæ* (first edition, 1706) went through ten editions in fifty years, and undoubtedly played a part in the transformation of English poetry in the first half of the century. The preface is largely an attack on what the writer considered the immoral tendencies of the poetry of his time; but it is also of critical interest as showing his realization of the imaginative quality of Hebrew literature, and as an attempt to break down the exclusive position held by classical subjects in the field of neo-classic poetry. In this respect the preface is both an echo of one aspect of the Ancients and Moderns controversy and an anticipation of the Romantic

recognition of Hebrew literature, which we associate especially
with Coleridge.

Mr Dennis. In *The Grounds of Criticism in Poetry* (1704.)

De la foy d'un Chrêtien. Boileau, *Art poétique*, iii. 199.

The French critic. Rapin, whose *Réflexions sur l'usage de l'Eloquence*
appeared in 1672.

p. 66. *Some of their best tragedies.* *E.g.*, Corneille's *Polyeucte* (1643), or
Racine's *Athalie* (1691).

Davideis. Abraham Cowley's unfinished epic, published in 1657.

The two Arthurs. Sir Richard Blackmore's epic, *Prince Arthur* (1695).
and the enlarged version of the poem (1697) entitled *King Arthur*.

Edward Young: from "On Lyric Poetry"

p. 66. Edward Young is now chiefly remembered for his very
popular poem, *The Complaint, or Night Thoughts on Life, Death and
Immortality* (1742–45); but he was also the author of tragedies,
satires, and odes, and the "Discourse on Ode," from which this
extract is taken, was prefixed to his *Ocean: an Ode* of 1728. This
essay touches on the nature of the Pindaric ode (much under discussion in this period) and emphasizes the need for 'fire' and
originality in poetry. The influence of 'Longinus' is clearly seen
in this essay, in which Young maintains that "dignity and spirit
ever suffer from scrupulous exactness." The last few lines quoted
anticipate clearly the note of the author's *Conjectures on Original
Composition* (see p. 90), though Young has not, in this earlier
preface, moved as far away from classical doctrine as he was to do
later on.

Edmund Burke: from "Of the Sublime and the Beautiful"

(For note on Burke's *Sublime and Beautiful* see p. 218 below.)

p. 68. Burke's theory of poetry is clearly linked with the views
expressed in the preceding essays in this section, and also with
Addison's paper in *The Spectator*, No. 416, on the power of words
over the imagination. See p. 103 above. The influence of
'Longinus' *On the Sublime* is again apparent.

These paragraphs are a further attempt to show the limitations
of the 'imitation' theory and advance the analysis of the emotional
value of words. Burke shows how, in poetry, words affect us as
much by the associations they arouse and the emotional stimuli
they provide as by their pictorial and logical values. He therefore

denies the classical doctrine (formulated again in the eighteenth century by the Abbé Du Bos) that poetry moves us principally by evoking clear images, and that it is, like painting, an art primarily concerned with the 'imitation' of nature. For Burke, ideas obscurely expressed, ideas of terror and sublimity beyond the reach of painting, exercise a far greater power over the imagination than clearly comprehended images, and are the chief source of the sublime in poetry.

In thus distinguishing between the functions of poetry and painting, and in opposing the imitation theory, Burke was making an important contribution to critical thought, and this was fully appreciated by Lessing in his analysis of the different spheres of poetry and the plastic arts in his *Laocoön* (1766). It must, however, be remembered that, in making this comparison, Burke wrote with seventeenth-century classical painting most in mind. Had he been writing some fifty years later his views on painting would undoubtedly have been modified by the new achievements of landscape painting and by the revival of interest that had taken place in the work of Michelangelo.

Animi motus, . . . "The tongue brings forth and interprets the movements of the mind."

p. 70. *Sanguine fœdantem* . . . "Making foul with blood the altar which he had himself consecrated." Virgil, *Æneid*, Book ii, l. 52.

Universe of death. Milton, *Paradise Lost*, ii, 618–622.

George Farquhar: from "Discourse upon Comedy"

p. 72. George Farquhar was born in Londonderry, but passed the adult years of his short life in London, where he worked as an actor and dramatist until his death, in circumstances of great poverty, in 1707. His two last plays, *The Recruiting Officer* (1706) and *The Beaux' Strategem* (1707) are the best remembered. Something of the vivacity that marks these plays is reflected in this *Discourse*.

Farquhar's line of argument against the critics and virtuosi may be paralleled in Pope's preface to the *Iliad* and in Hutcheson's *Inquiry*.

Vox populi. "The voice of the people is the voice of God." This saying is first found in Alcuin's *Admonitio ad Carolum Magnum* (c. 800 A.D.).

p. 73. *Alexander the Great*. Probably a reference to Nathaniel Lee's play *The Rival Queens, or the Death of Alexander the Great* (1677).

When Alexander fell a victim to the charms of Roxana, his wife Statira, whom he loved passionately, vowed to see him no more. Her vow was revoked on the banishment of Roxana, but Roxana took her revenge by stabbing Statira to death.

Mr Betterton. Thomas Betterton (1635–1710) was considered by Pepys "the best actor in the world." He was especially renowned for his rendering of Shakespearean rôles—Hamlet, Macbeth, and Mark Antony. See *The Tatler*, Nos. 1, 71, 167.

p. 74. *Nullum minus* . . . "The less cannot contain the greater." With Farquhar's arguments about the unities compare Johnson's discussion in the preface to Shakespeare. See pp. 84–89 above and the note on pp. 201–202.

p. 75. *Covent-Garden Church.* St Paul's, Covent Garden, still particularly associated, as in 1700, with the world of the theatre.

Will's Coffee-House. Situated in Russell Street, Covent Garden; the rendezvous of wits and men of letters in the latter years of the seventeenth century.

Joseph Addison: from "The Spectator"

p. 76. These two essays, in which there are clear echoes of 'Longinus,' are significant early statements on the nature of genius. Addison sees genius as attaining moments of beauty and sublimity beyond the reach of imitation; works of genius, he says, rise above the Rules, and in the last resort it is irrelevant to apply formal and authoritarian criticism to them. Pope writes in a similar vein in his preface to the *Iliad*, praising Homer for his "unequalled fire" and "amazing invention"—invention being the distinguishing feature of every great genius. It should be noted that Addison did not consider this view of genius irreconcilable with the neo-classical conception of art; the latter part of Paper 160 attempts to bridge the gap between the neo-classical and the Romantic lines of critical approach. The two kinds of genius to which Addison refers had been distinguished in similar terms by Shaftesbury, who referred to the first as "the natural and simple genius of antiquity," and to the second as "that which has its rise chiefly from the critical art itself and from more accurate inspection into the works of preceding masters."

Homer, Virgil, Old Testament. This view of the difference between Homer and Virgil was frequently expressed at this time; *e.g.*, by Pope, preface to the *Iliad*. With this recognition of the sublimity of the *Old Testament* compare the statement of Watts, p. 65 above.

p. 77. *Solomon*. Song of Solomon, chapter vii, verse 4.

Bienséance. Decorum or propriety. *Cf.* Boileau, *Art poétique*, iii, 119–123.

p. 78. *Longinus*. See Introduction, p. 20, and note on p. 191.

Quintilian. M. Fabius Quintilianus (A.D. 40–95), author of the most famous Latin treatise on rhetoric, *De Institutione Oratoria Libri XII.*

Dacier. André Dacier (1651–1722), a famous French classical scholar. His translation of Aristotle's *Poetics* (1692) was translated into English anonymously in 1705.

p. 80. *Gusto grande*. 'The grand style.' The word 'gusto,' which originally meant 'taste' (see note, p. 196 above), came later to signify 'style.'

Quorum æmular . . . "He fervently desires to emulate their carelessness rather than the ignoble scrupulousness of men of little genius." The quotation is from Terence's first play, *Andria*, Prologue, ll. 20–21 (166 B.C.).

Dr South. Dr Robert South (1634–1716), English divine.

Secundum artem. According to art or 'the rules.'

Pyrrhus's ring. Pyrrhus (318–272 B.C.) was King of Epirus and a noted warrior.

Pliny. Pliny the Elder (A.D. 23–79).

Samuel Johnson: from "The Rambler" and the preface to Shakespeare

p. 81. Johnson's preface claims for Shakespeare the poetic genius and superiority to the Rules which Pope's preface to the *Iliad* had claimed for Homer. It amplifies, in a piece of admirable prose, the briefer, but very significant, statements made in *The Rambler*, No. 156. In that essay Johnson discussed the Horatian rules of "three speaking personages" and of five acts as the recognized form of tragedy (*Ars poetica*, ll. 189–192). He also dealt with the unities of time and place, and carried the attack on these so-called 'rules' to its logical conclusion by showing that limits cannot be set to the play of imagination.

Dryden had been the first English critic to challenge the unities clearly, but even he, out of a mistaken idea of dramatic verisimilitude, had been prepared to attach some value to them. Johnson, though "frighted at his own temerity," as he says in the preface, sees the whole truth of the matter.

These passages owe a debt not only to Dryden's *Essay of*

Dramatic Poesy but also to Farquhar (see p. 74 above), and to Pope's preface to Shakespeare. Johnson was further indebted to the arguments put forward by Lord Kames in chapter xxiii of his *Elements of Criticism* (1762). Although Kames would not allow unbounded licence in the duration or extent of a dramatic action, and felt that he could not justify Shakespeare's *Winter's Tale*, he was convinced that the variety and wealth of substance that characterized modern drama could not be constricted within classical limits. He also pointed out that if our imagination can accept the stage itself, its scenery and effects, and the intervals that must occur in the representation of a play, we are not likely to be troubled by questions of the imaginary duration or location of the action of the drama. That these discussions were carried on into the sixties shows how long the notion of the unities held sway in English criticism.

Johnson's defence of tragi-comedy is, like his criticism of the unities, based on a psychological consideration of his subject. Most of his predecessors—Sidney, Ben Jonson, Milton, and even Dryden—had adopted the classical point of view, and as late as 1695 Dryden had spoken of tragi-comedy as "wholly Gothic," notwithstanding its success on the stage (*Parallel of Poetry and Painting*; cf. also *Essay of Dramatic Poesy*).

p. 82. *Voltaire . . . Cato.* The famous French writer Voltaire (1694–1778) was in England from 1726–29, and wrote his impressions in his *Lettres philosophiques sur les anglais* (1733). In this preface, however, Johnson is referring more directly to his *Du Théâtre anglais* (1761). Addison's tragedy *Cato*, written in imitation of formal classical tragedy, was produced in 1704.

A garden accurately formed. Both Pope and Addison use the same image. Pope (preface to the *Iliad*) refers to Homer's work as a wild Paradise, where if we cannot see all the beauties so distinctly as in an ordered garden, it is only because the number of them is infinitely greater.

p. 85. *Dragons of Medea.* Medea, having been deserted by Jason, murdered her two children and her rival, Glauce, daughter of Creon, King of Corinth, and fled to Athens in a chariot drawn by winged dragons.

p. 86. *Pharsalia.* In Thessaly; scene of the famous battle in which Cæsar defeated Pompey in 48 B.C.

Granicus. A river in the north-west of Asia Minor. Here Alexander the Great won the first of his three great victories over the

Persians in 334 B.C., and here Lucullus defeated Mithridates, in 73 B.C.

p. 87. *Mithridates.* Mithridates the Great (120–63 B.C.), King of Pontus, the most north-easterly part of Asia Minor, rebelled against Roman domination and was engaged in a series of campaigns against the Romans in Greece and Asia Minor between 89 B.C. and his death in 63 B.C.

Lucullus. One of the consuls in command of the Roman forces in the Third Mithridatic War, 74–67 B.C.

p. 89. *Non usque adeo . . .* "Length of time has not confused the highest and the lowest to such an extent, that the laws, if they had to be preserved by the voice of Metellus, would not prefer to be destroyed by Cæsar." Lucan, *Pharsalia*, iii. 138–140.

Edward Young: from "Conjectures on Original Composition"

p. 90. In this letter, addressed to Samuel Richardson the novelist, Young makes a bolder and more comprehensive statement of the view of genius suggested by Pope's preface to Homer and Johnson's preface to Shakespeare. While not seeking in any way to diminish the glory of the classics, he writes freely as a modern and a Romantic. He not only discusses the proper use to be made of classical models, but in the noble and eloquent conclusion of this passage foreshadows the development of historical criticism by showing how human genius evolves through the ages.

Elysium. Homer's happy land of notable heroes; in Hesiod the Isles of the Blest.

Tempe. The beautiful and romantic valley below Mount Olympus, in the north of Thessaly. The river Peneus flowed through this valley.

Armida's wand. Armida is an enchantress who figures in Tasso's *Gierusalemme Liberata*. She induces a number of Christian knights to follow her and transforms them into fishes (cantos iv, x). The description of her palace and garden (cantos xv–xvi) provided suggestions for Spenser's 'bower of Acrasia' in Book II of the *Faerie Queene*.

Meo sum Pauper . . . "I am poor in money." Horace.

p. 92. *Hercules.* The allegory of the 'Choice of Hercules' (between Virtue and Pleasure) is found in Xenophon's *Memorabilia*, II, i, 21.

The cynic. The Athenian philosopher Diogenes (412–323 B.C.), who asked Alexander the Great not to stand between him and the sunshine.

Helicon. The fountains of the Muses (Aganippe and Hippocrene) were situated in the Helicon range of mountains in Bœotia. This range was sacred to Apollo and the Muses.

p. 93. *Stat contra . . .* "Your page lies opposite and says, 'Thou art a thief!'"—Martial.

p. 94. *Nemo unquam . . .* "There was never a great man who was not possessed of some divine inspiration."—Cicero.

Learning and genius. The contrast which Young draws between learning and genius—and, indeed, the whole of this portion of the letter—echoes the opening of Pope's preface to his translation of the *Iliad.*

Jura negat . . . "He denies that laws were made for him; there is nothing he does not accomplish."

Natos sine . . . "Flowers produced without the sowing of seed."—Ovid.

p. 95. *Kick the beam.* "Weigh lighter."—Milton, *Paradise Lost,* iv. 1004.

Joseph Addison: from "The Spectator"

p. 96. These essays "On the Pleasures of the Imagination" were undoubtedly among the *Spectator* papers which had most influence on the thought of their time and on succeeding critical developments. They not only provided the basic material for Akenside's verse treatise *The Pleasures of Imagination* (1744), but stimulated much more important writers in this field, such as Burke and Kant.

It is true that Addison's views were sometimes limited by the taste of his age, as for example in his comparison (in No. 415), so derogatory to the Gothic, of the architecture of the Pantheon with that of the medieval cathedrals. Sometimes, again, he tried to see truth in two directions at once, as in his account of the relationship between the beauty of art and the beauty of nature (No. 414) or between untamed nature and formalized landscape. But in spite of these limitations, there is no doubt that Addison gave a new form to the thought of the time on the nature and functions of imagination, and made a positive contribution to the theory of beauty and sublimity. The psychological theory on which the essays are based is not original; it is largely derived from Locke, as is obvious from No. 413 (*cf.* No. 62)—but the papers are full of original suggestions and flashes of insight into the heart of the writer's subject. It is especially interesting to see how much other writers in the century owe to Addison's conception of natural sublimity and its effect upon the mind (No. 412), to his analysis of

the pleasure of tragedy and the æsthetic delight which may be
given by the representation in art of things terrible or painful or
ugly in themselves (No. 418), and to his analysis of "the fairy
way of writing" (No. 419). Burke's debt to the first two papers
mentioned, and Hurd's to the last, are obvious.

Our sight. The limitation of Addison's æsthetic theory to images
derived from sight must be borne in mind throughout.

p. 97. *Imagination or Fancy.* The equivalence of these two terms as
used by Addison in 1712 is noteworthy. (See note on p. 223.)

Primary and secondary pleasures of imagination. It is obvious from what
follows that by "primary pleasures" Addison does not mean
merely sensuous appreciation, but the ideal or spiritual significance of beauty, novelty, or grandeur, and that the "secondary
pleasures" also include the primary. The conception is similar to
that of Ruskin's "typical beauty" in *Modern Painters*, Vol. II.
Coleridge's distinction between primary and secondary imagination is differently founded.

p. 98. *Greatness, Novelty, Beauty.* Addison's enlargement of the
æsthetic sphere is interesting, and his remarks on grandeur—
which probably owe something to 'Longinus' and to Boileau—
undoubtedly influenced Burke and Kant in their treatment of the
sublime. Addison's idea of the æsthetic quality of novelty was
probably developed from a hint given by Hobbes. This notion
has made little appeal; though as developed by Addison it has
some kinship with Pater's definition of Romanticism as "strangeness added to beauty," and is also a foreshadowing of the feeling
for the picturesque which grew as the century advanced. The
paper No. 412 shows that novelty does not merely signify the
presence of what is new, but connotes also life and movement.

It is noteworthy that, in treating of beauty, Burke adopts
Addison's division of his subject, dealing first with beauty as
related with sexual attraction, and then with beauty of form.

p. 101. *Secondary pleasures of imagination.* The first sentence of paper
No. 416 is obscure to modern ears. The distinction between
primary and secondary pleasures is more clearly put in No. 411.
(See p. 97.)

p. 102. *Pleasure of comparison.* Compare Aristotle on imitation,
Poetics, iv. 1–5, and *Spectator*, No. 418.

p. 103. *The poet seems to get the better of Nature.* Compare Sidney's
Apologie for Poetrie: "Nature never set forth the earth in so rich
tapestry as divers poets have done," and Burke's more penetrating
analysis on p. 69 above.

p. 104. *Milton's Paradise and Hell*. Few would agree with Addison here. He seems misled by superficial logic.

p. 105. *Informe cadaver* . . . "A hideous corpse is dragged forward: they are unable to satisfy their feelings with gazing at the terrible eyes, the face and shaggy breast of the half-man, half-beast, and the once-fiery jaws."—Virgil, *Æneid*, viii, 264–267.

p. 107. *The fairy way of writing*. See note on p. 192.

Sylvis deducti . . . "In my opinion the Fauns, brought from the woods, should be wary of wantoning too much with trifling verses, as if they were born in the highway and almost belonged to the market-place."—Horace, *Ars Poetica*, ll. 244–246.

The Rehearsal. The farcical comedy (1672) by George Villiers, second Duke of Buckingham, in which the authors of contemporary heroic tragedies are satirized in the person of Mr Bayes the poet, who probably represents Davenant.

p. 109. *Fame*. Virgil, *Æneid*, iv. 173.

Sin and Death. Milton, *Paradise Lost*, ii. 648–883.

p. 110. *The new philosophy*. "Natural science."

Joseph Warton: from "An Essay on the Genius and Writings of Pope"

p. 112. Joseph Warton was the son of Thomas Warton the elder (Professor of Poetry at Oxford; died 1745) and brother of Thomas Warton the younger, the historian of English poetry (see Introduction, pp. 45–46). At Winchester he was a schoolfellow of the poet Collins, and he later became headmaster of this school. The first volume of his *Essay* on Pope was published in 1756, the second in 1782. He edited a complete edition of the poet's works in 1797.

In common with his father and brother, Joseph Warton contributed a good deal to the growth of 'pre-Romantic' elements in the poetry of his age, even if in his later years he tended to become more classical in taste and outlook. It is significant that the *Essay* is dedicated to Young. The passage quoted comes from this Dedication.

Fontenelle. French philosopher and scientist, 1657–1757. He also wrote poems and plays.

La Motte-Houdard. French tragedian and critic, 1672–1731.

p. 113. *La Bruyère*. 1645–96; his famous *Caractères* appeared in 1688.

Richard Hurd: from "Letters on Chivalry and Romance"

p. 113. Hurd was a contemporary and friend of Gray and William Mason at Cambridge. His first important work was his edition of Horace's *Ars Poetica*, with commentary (1749). His *Moral and Political Dialogues* were published in 1759, and the *Letters on Chivalry and Romance* followed three years later as an appendix to the Third Dialogue. Hurd was made Bishop of Lichfield and Coventry in 1774, and translated to Worcester in 1781.

In this tenth and last of the *Letters* Hurd boldly insists on the supreme value of "poetic truth," and claims that truth to the laws of imagination is more powerful in art than "truth to nature." This is an interesting attempt to give a complete justification of 'Romantic' art.

Liars by profession. The poets had been accused by Plato (*Republic*, Book II) of telling lies and corrupting men's minds: but Aristotle (*Poetics*, xxiv) had shown how the impossible or the marvellous in poetry was to be defended. Renaissance critics, such as Sidney, had again felt the need to defend poetry against the charge of falsifying the truth; and the question, though not often explicitly discussed, remained in the background of critical thought in the neo-classic period, when the marvellous and the fantastic in poetry were suspect, and stress was laid on poetry's social and didactic functions.

p. 114. *O! who can tell* . . . Spenser, *Faerie Queene*, I, ii, 10.

Non hic Centauros . . . "Not here will you find Centaurs, Gorgons and Harpies; our page presents Man." Martial, *Epigrams*, x, 4.

p. 115. *Incredulus odi.* Horace, *Ars Poetica*, l. 188: "Whatever you show me of this sort I am incredulous of and therefore dislike."

Segnius irritant . . . Horace, *Ars Poetica*, ll. 180 et seq. "Things which pass into the mind through the ears make a tardier impression than those which are brought before the eyes and which the spectator himself witnesses."

Multaque tolles . . . This continues the quotation: "and you receive many things from sight before they are eloquently narrated."

Absens facundia. "Recital of actions not immediately witnessed." The phrase is made by analogy with Horace's *facundia praesens* (*Ars Poetica*, l. 184).

p. 116. *Tasso.* Torquato Tasso (1544–95), author of *Gierusalemme Liberata.*

Magnanima mensogna . . . "When is the truth so beautiful that it can be preferred to splendid lies?"

p. 117. *Celestial intervention.* Compare Dennis's statements in *The Advancement and Reformation of Modern Poetry* on the force of religious inspiration in epic poetry. See p. 62 above.

Henriade. Voltaire's heroic poem exalting Henri IV (1723).

Gondibert. Sir William Davenant's unfinished epic (1651) which tells a chivalric story set in Lombardy.

Edmund Burke: from "On Taste"

p. 118. Burke, who approaches his subject from the psychological standpoint, sets out to show that there can be a standard of taste, and that taste must include judgment and knowledge as well as sensibility. It is this emphasis on judgment that chiefly brings this essay into close relationship with classical doctrine. It may be that Burke's view of his subject is confused at some points, but his conclusions represent a real advance in the theory of taste—chiefly because he perceives that taste is not a separate faculty of the mind, but a particular mode of the harmonious operation of sensibility, imagination, and judgment. (See note on p. 224.)

This essay was prefixed to the second edition of *The Sublime and the Beautiful* (1759). With Burke's treatment of this subject compare David Hume's essay *Of the Standard of Taste* (1757).

p. 120. *Horace.* See *Ars Poetica*, ll. 309–322.

Samuel Johnson: from "Rasselas" and the preface to Shakespeare

p. 124. These passages form an interesting late statement of the neo-classical position. They emphasize the part played by reason in poetic creation, and insist on poetry's ethical purpose. They have also the positive merit of stressing the artist's need of knowledge (*cf.* Fielding, *Tom Jones*, XIV, i) to which weaker 'Romantic' writers have at all times attached too little importance—though it is true that the value of this emphasis is somewhat diminished, from the æsthetic point of view, by Johnson's insistence on the *general* nature of such knowledge.

These extracts do not, however, give by any means a complete picture of Johnson's critical outlook, other aspects of which are seen in Section III of this book.

Johnson's ethical story on the 'Choice of Life'—*Rasselas, Prince of Abyssinia*—from which the first passage is taken, makes little pretence to local colour or characterization. Imlac, who tells the story of his mind in the early chapters, is to some extent an idealized portrait of Johnson himself. In this dissertation on poetry in chapter x Imlac stresses the need for the poet to have a wide knowledge of man and nature, and shows that in such knowledge he must advance from the particular to the 'specific' —*i.e.*, in modern terms, the 'general.'

Sir Joshua Reynolds: from "Discourses"

p. 126. Reynolds remains, in the opinion of many, the greatest of English portrait-painters. He was the first President of the Royal Academy; and a member of the famous "Club" to which Johnson, Goldsmith, and Garrick belonged.

Reynolds's *Discourses* link the discussion of taste and genius with the theory of beauty and show how the classical conception of art was still applied in painting in the latter part of the century.

Reynolds deals very fully with the relationship between genius and the Rules and with the nature of the 'grand style.' His conception of beauty is an attempt to bridge the gulf between subjective and objective theories; beauty is to him at once the ideal to which Nature tends and that which pleases man's imagination; it is able to fulfil these two functions simultaneously because of the harmony which exists between Nature and the mind of man.

On all these topics the *Discourses* develop and illustrate ideas which Reynolds first expounded in three papers contributed to *The Idler* in 1759 (Nos. 76, 79, 82).

In elaborating his view of art Reynolds begins by showing the insufficiency of the neo-classic imitation theory. This, according to him, explains only the primitive appeal of works of art, and the nature of its lowest forms. The Rules of art, again, and rational explanation of æsthetic phenomena, have only a limited value. The artist must penetrate more deeply; he must study the principles of Nature and of the human mind; the laws of Nature and of imagination must be his guide. He will thus come to perceive 'ideal beauty,' and will see the need for working in the 'grand style'—the style in which Michelangelo is superior to all other masters.

While showing the limitations of the Rules, however, Reynolds was not carried away by the exaggerated notion of 'genius' current in his time. He never ceased to value technique, and continually stressed the importance of the study of classical masters. In this respect Reynolds became more strictly classical in outlook as the years advanced.

O

Phidias. The greatest of the Greek sculptors of the age of Pericles. Born *c.* 490 B.C.

Proclus. Athenian neo-Platonic philosopher, A.D. 410–485.

p. 127. *Great style, genius, taste.* Reynolds's use of the three terms as equivalent is noteworthy.

p. 128. *Enthusiasm, reason.* This antithesis has taken the place of Pope's opposition of 'wit' and 'judgment.'

Care in digesting, methodizing. Reynolds is convinced, like Hurd and Young, that genius cannot be explained by rules; but is less willing than they to disparage the value of reason and method.

p. 130. *Bacon.* See Essay xliii, *Of Beauty.* Albrecht Dürer, the great German artist (1471–1528), wrote a book entitled *De symmetria partium in rectis formis humanorum corporum.* Bacon attributed to the Greek painter Apelles what Cicero (*De Inventione,* II, i, 1) says of Zeuxis—that, wishing to paint Helen as an ideal woman for the temple of Venus at Crotona, he based his work on the finest features of five beautiful maidens.

p. 131. *Imitation.* Note that this term has a different meaning here from that which it bears in the previous discourse, where it sig-fies the copying of nature.

p. 134. *Promethean fire.* Prometheus was originally a god of fire, but was later regarded as the god who had taught man not only the use of fire, but also architecture and all other arts. It is thus that Æschylus presents him in his trilogy, and Shelley develops this conception still further in his *Prometheus Unbound.*

Genius and taste. This explanation of terms should be noted.

p. 135. *Nature.* There is a clear link between Reynolds's doctrine and earlier neo-classic theory. But, as is obvious from the rest of the *Discourse,* Reynolds is not arguing for a limited and merely realistic truth to Nature. His conception of 'Nature' is much more profound than that of Pope. Nature is here used as the 'ideal' or the 'typical.'

p. 138. *Taking particular living objects for nature.* This is developed in *Discourse XIII.*

Alexander Pope: from the preface to Shakespeare

p. 143. *Ben Jonson's use of the Chorus.* Notable examples are the prologues to the London version of *Every Man in his Humour,* and to *Every Man out of his Humour.*

Grex. The company of actors.

Model of the Ancients. Pope was ignorant of earlier plays in classical form, such as *Ralph Roister Doister* and *Gammer Gurton's Needle*, and he overlooked *Gorbuduc* (1561).

To judge of Shakespeare by Aristotle's rules. Nicholas Rowe had already made this point in almost identical terms in the preface to his edition of Shakespeare of 1709: "But as Shakespeare lived under a kind of mere light of Nature, and had never been made acquainted with the regularity of those written precepts, so it would be hard to judge him by a law he knew nothing of."

Ancient, majestic piece of Gothic architecture. This interesting comparison was repeated by Hurd (Letter VIII, p. 146 above); it is a significant illustration of Pope's Romantic sympathies.

Richard Hurd: from "Letters on Chivalry and Romance"

p. 144. *Two systems.* I.e., the classic and the Gothic or Romantic.

Gothic and Classic in Tasso. See the passage quoted from Letter, X p. 116 above, and the note on p. 207.

Ariosto. Ludovico Ariosto (1474–1533). Spenser himself acknowledged that he hoped to emulate and perhaps to "overgo" the *Orlando Furioso* of Ariosto. He owed much to Ariosto, both in detail and in the conception of a chivalric romance built on epic lines; but Hurd is right in emphasizing the essential differences between the two poets.

Milton's favourite subject. As late as 1643 Milton was still contemplating the writing of a drama or poem on the subject of Arthur. His interest in the legends of chivalry is seen in many later passages—*e.g.*, *Paradise Lost*, i, 579–587, 779–788; *Paradise Regained*, iii, 338–341.

p. 145. *Amadis.* Garcia de Montalvo wrote the romance of *Amadis de Gaula* in Spanish, in four parts, in the second half of the fifteenth century, but the story of this romance was current in Portuguese or Spanish a century earlier. It was translated into French in 1540, and became well known throughout western Europe. Cervantes makes interesting references to it (see, for example, *Don Quixote*, Part I, chapter vi).

Sir Launcelot of the Lake. Sir Lancelot was the subject of a French romance of the thirteenth century. In England his story was first fully developed by Malory in the *Morte d'Arthur*.

Chaucer's unfinished story. "The Squire's Tale," referred to in the passage of Milton's *Il Penseroso* here quoted.

p. 146. *Gothic structure and Grecian rules.* Compare Pope, preface to Shakespeare, p. 143 above.

p. 147. *Matthieu de Couci.* This French chronicler (1420–1483) is now known as Matthieu d'Escouchy. His chronicle covers the years 1444–64.

Olivier de la Marche. French chronicler and poet (1426–1502), now chiefly remembered for his *Memoirs*.

Monstrelet. Enguerrand de Monstrelet (*c.* 1400–53), French chronicler. His work deals with the period 1400–44, and may be regarded as a sequel to that of Froissart.

Letter to Sir Walter Raleigh on the *Faerie Queene*, January 23, 1589.

p. 148. *Unity of design, not of action.* This is a better argument than that put forward by John Hughes, who claimed that the character of Prince Arthur gave unity to the poem (see his edition of Spenser's *Works*, 1715); but even Hurd does not realize that the unity of the poem is chiefly one of atmosphere and of the coherence of the poet's imaginative world.

Gothic design in gardening. Hurd seems to be thinking of the radiating avenues or glades that had their origin in the French style of the late seventeenth century. These did not belong to the Gothic tradition, and Hurd's illustration, while it fits his immediate purpose well enough, is therefore rather curious.

p. 149. *Kent.* See note on p. 216.

In liete aspetto . . . Tasso, *Gierusalemme Liberata*, xvi, 9:

> These windings passed, the garden gates unfold,
> And the fair Eden meets their glad survey,—
> Still waters, moving crystals, sands of gold,
> Herbs, thousand flowers, rare shrubs, and mosses grey;
> Sunshiny hillocks, shady vales; woods gay,
> And grottos gloomy, in one view combined,
> Presented were; and what increased their play
> Of pleasure at the prospect, was, to find
> Nowhere the happy art that had the whole designed.
>
> *(translated by J. H. Wiffen)*

Lord Shaftesbury: from "Characteristics"

p. 150. For note on Shaftesbury, see p. 194.

Nature. The increased awareness of the beauty and spiritual value of nature began to be revealed quite early in eighteenth-century poetry, as is shown, for example, by Lady Winchelsea's *Nocturnal Reverie*, but the revolution in garden-design was well under way, and the appreciation of landscape painting was widespread, before an interest in natural scenery became universal, or nature a frequent subject in poetry.

Joseph Addison: from "The Spectator"

p. 150. The essayists Shaftesbury, in his *Characteristics*, Addison, in this essay and in *The Tatler*, No. 161, and Pope, in *The Guardian*, No. 173, did much to break the vogue of the formal garden, and Pope's own garden at Twickenham was a good example of transitional design.

p. 151. *English Gardens.* Addison is here contrasting the typical English formal garden with the layout of the much larger 'park' of Continental noble houses, and taking no account of the formal plan on which such estates (*e.g.*, Versailles) were commonly based. Later, the English landscape garden became the subject of imitation abroad.

China. Sir William Temple had referred to the natural or irregular gardens of China in his essay *Upon the Gardens of Epicurus*, 1690. Horace Walpole added to the second edition of his *History of the Modern Taste in Gardening* a long note attempting to show that French writers were in error in assuming that what was later known as *le jardin anglais* was largely imitated from Chinese example; and it is true that the natural garden is not un-English; but Addison's essay shows that, while the formal garden was still in vogue here, the idea of naturalness was indeed associated with China.

A word in their language. 'Sharawadgi.' This word (also written 'sharawaggi') is of unknown origin; it is not Chinese; it is first found in English in Sir William Temple's *Gardens of Epicurus* (1690): "The Chinese ... have a particular word to express it; *i.e.*, 'studied irregularity': and where they find it hit their eye at first sight, they say the *Sharawadgi* is fine or is admirable."

p. 152. *Marks of the Scissors.* The art of 'topiary' flourished especially in the William and Mary and Queen Anne periods. Compare Walpole's essay, p. 158 above. A few examples of topiary gardens remain—*e.g.*, at Blenheim Palace.

Parterre. A terrace or level ornamental portion of the garden, in which elaborate geometrical patterns were formed by flower-beds cut in the turf or framed by dwarf hedges, with gravel paths between them. The formal pattern was emphasized by the different colours of the beds of flowers and sometimes by the use of coloured gravels. A few such parterres are preserved both in this country—for example, at Blenheim, Hatfield, and Holkham —and on the Continent.

Horace Walpole: from a Letter to Richard West

p. 152. It was not until the days of the Wartons, Gray, and Walpole that descriptions of, or reflections upon, natural scenery began to figure frequently in literature.

Addison's *Remarks on Several Parts of Italy* (and Switzerland) *in the Years* 1701, 1702, 1703, are entirely lacking in landscape description and in any real feeling for the Alps or Apennines; the notes describe buildings and monuments, remains and curiosities, people and customs, trade and agriculture, but do not give more on scenery than very brief touches, such as "pleasant country." The same is true of Dr Johnson's *Journey to the Western Islands* (1775).

The only writer of this period in whom the sight of the Alps aroused something of the feeling that mountain scenery inspired in the Romantics was John Dennis. In a letter written from Turin on October 25, 1688, describing the crossing of the Alps, Dennis speaks of the sense of power and sublimity which these "ruins of Nature" conveyed to him, and refers to the mountains as "Nature's extravagancies," "bold strokes . . . wrought in a fury."

Horace Walpole, the fourth son of Sir Robert Walpole, was one of the leading men of fashion and culture in the mid-eighteenth century, and intimately connected with the literary and artistic movements of his day. On leaving Cambridge he undertook the 'Grand Tour' with the poet Gray for his companion. He sat in Parliament from 1741–67, but literature, art, and society were the chief occupations of his life. In 1747 he bought the house at Strawberry Hill, Twickenham (described in his lively letter of June 12, 1753, to Sir Horace Mann), and, in addition to gathering together curios and *objets d'art*, set up a printing-press there, on which were printed Gray's *The Bard* and *The Progress of Poesy*, and some of his own works—the *Catalogue of Royal and Noble Authors*, *Anecdotes of Painting in England*, and the *Catalogue of Engravers in England*. Walpole's letters throw much light on the society and events of his day, while his fantastic Gothic novel, *The Castle of Otranto* (1764), inaugurated a new vein in English fiction.

Walpole's letter, and the first two extracts of those of Gray which follow, were written when the two friends were making the 'Grand Tour,' and journeying down through France into Italy. *Richard West*. A friend of Gray and of Walpole at Eton. He went on

to Oxford and then to study law in London, but died of con-
sumption in 1742, at the age of 26.

Thomas Gray: from his Letters

p. 153. *The Grande Chartreuse*. The monastery of the Grande
Chartreuse is situated in the French Alps, near Grenoble.

p. 154. *St Bruno*. Founder of the monastery in 1086.

Netley Abbey. The ruins of this Cistercian monastery stand near
Southampton. Gray had visited the abbey before, in July 1755.
The descriptive phrases in this letter recall the *Elegy* and Collins's
Ode to Evening.

"*Too full of gauds*." Shakespeare, *King John*, III, iii, 3.

p. 155. *Journal-Letter* on the Lakes. This journal was written during
Gray's tour of the Lakes in 1769, and was sent to his friend Dr
Wharton, of Darlington, who was prevented by illness from
accompanying him.

p. 156. *The glass*. The "Claude-glass" or "Claude Lorraine glass,"
was a fashionable device with travellers of this time. By looking
at the reflection of a landscape in this darkened or coloured and
slightly convex hand-mirror, they got an impression of the scene
in subdued tones and somewhat concentrated as in a painting.

p. 157. "*Dark to me and silent . . .*" Milton, *Samson Agonistes*, ll.
86–89.

Horace Walpole: from "History of the Modern Taste in Gardening"

p. 157. Walpole's essay, which may have been written at any time
between 1750 and 1770, was first printed at Strawberry Hill in
the last volume (1771) of his *Anecdotes of Painting in England*. The
second edition was printed in 1782 under the title *The History of
the modern taste in gardening*.

At the time that Walpole's essay appeared the Rev. William
Mason was writing his verse treatise on the same subject, *The
English Garden, in Four Books* (1772–82). Mason's first book
covers, in blank verse, much the same ground as that of Walpole's
essay, and adopts a similar line of criticism.

p. 158. *Succedaneum to nature*. That is, a substitute for nature.

Canals. As, for example, at Hampton Court or Wrest Park, Bedfordshire.

Tricks of Waterworks. Tricks of this kind were occasionally used in gardens of great houses. They may be compared with the fake hermits who were kept in some of the Romantic gardens of the succeeding period.

Parterres embroidered. See note on p. 213.

Shears. See note on "marks of the scissors," p. 213 above.

p. 159. *Quincunx etoile.* Clusters of trees planted in the pattern of the five of dominoes or of a star.

Each alley has a brother . . . Pope, *Moral Essays*, Epistle IV, 117–118. Compare Pope's essay in *The Guardian*, No. 173.

Bridgman. Charles Bridgeman (died 1738), royal gardener from about 1720. He led the revolt against formal gardening. He designed Kensington Gardens, and the Serpentine, the royal garden at Richmond, and the gardens at Stowe.

Guardian, No. 173. Pope's plea for the natural garden.

Gubbins. The ancient manor of Gubbins, or More Hall, at North Mimms, Hertfordshire, was sold in 1836. The house was demolished and the grounds incorporated in the neighbouring Brookmans Park.

p. 160. *The ha! ha!* This seems to be the correct explanation of the origin of this term to denote a sunk fence; but in France the word was used in connexion with military fortification in the seventeenth century.

Houghton. Sir Robert Walpole's estate in Norfolk, a dozen miles N.E. of King's Lynn. The mansion was built in 1722–35, and was especially famous for its fine collection of pictures.

Kent. William Kent (1684–1748), painter, sculptor, architect, and landscape gardener. He was best known as an architect (see Introduction, p. 31), but was also consulted by people of wealth and fashion on all matters of decoration and furnishing. As a gardener he gave practical examples of the principles laid down in Pope's fourth *Epistle*, and, as Walpole points out (p. 161), was skilful in introducing architectural works, "temples," monuments, etc., into his landscape compositions.

p. 161. *The gentle stream was taught to serpentize.* The serpentine line, taken by Hogarth, in his *Analysis of Beauty* (1753), as the type of essential beauty, was adopted in landscape gardening even before it won its place in Rococo architecture and interior design.

p. 162. *A new creation.* The English parklands of the nineteenth century were, indeed, largely the creation of the landscape-gardeners of the preceding age, and it is difficult for us to realize how greatly the face of the countryside was changed in this period.

Uvedale Price: from "An Essay on the Picturesque"

p. 162. The full title of this essay is: *An Essay on the Picturesque, as compared with the Sublime and Beautiful: and on the Use of studying Pictures, for the Purpose of improving real Landscape.*

Price was educated at Eton and Christ Church, Oxford, and was something of a scholar; but his main interests were in agriculture and gardening. He continued the improvement of his family estate at Foxley, Herefordshire, and was the author of several essays on landscape gardening and on the picturesque. In these writings he carried the criticism of garden design one stage further than Walpole and Mason. He pleaded for greater naturalness and variety, and considered that Kent and Brown applied the principle of rounded masses and undulating lines too mechanically. He would have the landowner carry out his 'improvements' according to his own knowledge of the countryside and of landscape painting, leaving the naturally picturesque and romantic qualities of the landscape as far as possible untouched.

Mr Brown. Lancelot ("Capability") Brown, 1715–83. See Introduction, p. 30, and note on p. 192.

p. 163. *Mr Walpole.* See p. 159.

Mr Mason. The English Garden, in Four Books (1772–82).

A professed improver. At this time the best known was Brown's greatest successor, Humphry Repton. He was criticized by Price, and more bitterly by Richard Payne Knight, for his support of Brown's principles. Whereas Price and Knight aimed at greater freedom and picturesqueness than Brown, Repton favoured some return to formality in the parts of a garden adjacent to the house.

From his favourite masters in painting. See Introduction, p. 29.

Lord Shaftesbury: from "Characteristics"

p. 164. For note on Shaftesbury, see p. 194.

Shaftesbury's philosophy was an attempt to bring the moral and the æsthetic into close relationship. Some of his critics thought, indeed, that he made moral virtue too much a matter of taste. (See the extract from Burke on p. 174.)

In his æsthetic essays his view is that beauty, whether physical or spiritual, springs from inward perfection, and that the first essential for the artist who aims at presenting human life truly is to possess powers of moral and spiritual perception.

p. 166. *Venus.* In this sense the word means 'charm' or 'attraction.' This use of the word seems to have been short-lived.

Francis Hutcheson: from "An Inquiry into the Original of our Ideas of Beauty and Virtue"

p. 167. Hutcheson was born in Ulster and educated in Glasgow, where he was Professor of Moral Philosophy from 1729–46. He was much influenced by the thought of Shaftesbury, and worked out a theory of man's moral sense, with particular emphasis on the æsthetic aspect of virtue. The basis of his æsthetic is that man possesses a natural or innate sense of beauty and harmony; this sense Hutcheson identifies with Addison's 'imagination.'

Hutcheson makes an important contribution to æsthetic philosophy in stressing the *immediacy* of our perceptions of beauty and harmony.

p. 169. *Some objects are immediately the occasions of this pleasure of beauty.* An interesting anticipation of the emphasis that Kant was to place on the disinterestedness of the æsthetic sense. *Cf.* Addison, *Spectator*, No. 411 (p. 98 above).

p. 171. *Uniformity amidst variety.* A notion with a long history in the doctrine of formal beauty. Aristotle saw beauty of form as consisting in order and symmetry. Vitruvius, in his *De Architectura* (20–11 B.C.), gave a fuller exposition of proportion, harmony, and symmetry.

p. 174. *Natural sense of beauty.* Hutcheson attempts throughout to 'clear the ground' in his subject, and to isolate æsthetic experience from morality, custom, association of ideas, etc. In this he was followed by Burke, but others of his contemporaries and successors took opposite views. Thus Hume found the essence of our sense of beauty and deformity in ideas of pleasure and pain respectively, and Alison, at the end of the century, based his æsthetic on a theory of expression and association of ideas.

Edmund Burke: from "Of the Sublime and the Beautiful"

p. 174. After graduating at Trinity College, Dublin, Burke came to London to study law, but the subject had little attraction for him, and he spent much of his time in travel and in literary study. He became acquainted with Garrick and other literary men, and began to write as a means of supplementing the allowance he received from his family. His first publications were *A Vindication of Natural Society* and the treatise on the *Sublime and the Beautiful*, both published in 1756. This latter work had been begun before Burke was nineteen—which may account for the inequality of the essay, and for the repetitions that occur in it.

In spite of its crudities, however, the work marks a real advance in æsthetic inquiry. Burke was opposed to idealist and moralistic conceptions of beauty, and attempted to give a physiological and psychological explanation of æsthetic experience. He thus opened up a field of inquiry which had not been more than hinted at by his predecessors, Addison and Hume. To both these writers, however, and especially to Addison, Burke owed much, and his essay should be read against the background of the *Spectator* papers, Nos. 411–418.

Burke performed an even greater service to æsthetic theory in recognizing the sublime as an æsthetic category distinct from beauty, and in making a psychological analysis of the sentiment it inspires. Addison (see p. 98 above) and Hutcheson had, indeed, seen that grandeur made an appeal similar to that of beauty, but not identical with it; and in them, as first in Boileau, the 'sublime' had come to mean not merely elevation of style (as in earlier seventeenth-century writers) but grandeur of thought and emotion. But Burke carried the analysis of sublimity into greater detail and initiated a much deeper study of the emotional bearings of our experience of the sublime.

The value and originality of Burke's analysis are not diminished by the fact that other writers in this time were also considering this subject. For example, Richard West (1716–42) and Thomas Ashton (1716–75), the friends of Gray and Walpole, discussed in an exchange of letters on the sublime in 1740 how far sublimity was a matter of expression and how far of passion, and West particularly was getting close to Burke's stand-point.

The popularity of Burke's essay is indicated by the fact that the book reached its eighth edition within twenty years, and that it was translated into German in 1773 and into French in 1803.

p. 174. *Application of beauty to virtue.* Aimed, no doubt, at Shaftesbury. See p. 165 above.

p. 178. *Whose neck is clothed with thunder* . . . Job, xxxix, 19–24.

p. 179. *Infinite divisibility of matter. Cf.* Addison, p. 111 above.

Archibald Alison: from "On Taste"

p. 180. Alison was the son of a Provost of Edinburgh, but was educated in Glasgow, where he was a friend of Dugald Stewart, later famous as a philosopher. He went on to Oxford, and was ordained in the Church of England; he began his ministry in England, but moved back to Edinburgh in 1800.

Alison accepted neither the empirical theory of beauty as a quality in objects which could be analysed, nor the theory which looked on beauty as springing from an interior sense; but, developing suggestions found in Beattie's *Dissertations Moral and Critical* (1783), maintained that the sentiment of beauty was produced by trains of ideas arising from objects associated in our minds with simple emotions.

Alison's theory had considerable influence, and was given greater currency by Francis Jeffrey in the *Edinburgh Review* (May 1811) and in the article on "Beauty" written for the *Encyclopædia Britannica* (sixth edition, 1824). The relationships between his view of nature and Wordsworth's is obvious, and there is a clear link between his doctrine of beauty and that of Ruskin in *Modern Painters*, in spite of Ruskin's rejection of the association theory.

William Gilpin: from "Three Essays: on Picturesque Beauty, on Picturesque Travel, and on Sketching Landscape"

p. 184.   William Gilpin was born in Carlisle, and, after graduating at Oxford, was ordained in the Church of England. For nearly thirty years from 1748, however, he kept a school at Cheam, in Surrey. He was a man of an original and practical turn of mind, a reformer in education, and keen to widen and improve the social life of his parish. His school vacations were spent in sketching-tours, and these provided the materials for the descriptive travel books he published in the eighties and nineties. These volumes were very popular: for example, the *Observations on the River Wye* (1780) went into five editions before the end of the century, besides being translated into French. The *Tour in Cumberland and Westmorland* (1786) was translated into both French and German.

In his treatment of the picturesque Gilpin follows Burke's empirical method, and in the first part of his book examines the effect of roughness (which he believes to be the essence of the picturesque) in portrait-painting, landscape painting, scenery, animal life, statuary, colour, light and shade, etc. In the second part, which is an essay on picturesque travel, he writes of the picturesque in nature, and classifies picturesque objects or scenes as beautiful or sublime. The picturesque does not lie for him in the curious and fantastic elements of nature, but in natural scenery, including effects of atmosphere and living forms, "examined by the rules of painting." The word 'picturesque' thus has for Gilpin much of its literal meaning, and for this reason he does not attempt to differentiate absolutely between the beautiful and the picturesque or the picturesque and the sublime; he can still write of "picturesque beauty."

p. 184. *Mr Burke. Of the Sublime and Beautiful*, Part III, Section xiv.

Uvedale Price: from "An Essay on the Picturesque"

p. 185. For a note on Uvedale Price, see p. 217.

Price tells us that his *Essay* was begun before Gilpin's book was published, but it is evident that his interest in the picturesque was greatly stimulated by Gilpin, He follows Burke and Gilpin in his view of beauty and sublimity, but attempts to distinguish the picturesque from these qualities much more sharply than Gilpin, even though he admits that the picturesque may be combined with both beauty and sublimity. According to Price, the picturesque consists in 'roughness and sudden variation, with irregularity'; it is not dependent on any relationship with painting. By freeing the picturesque from this dependency Price opens up the possibility of a wider field of speculation.

That most original work. Burke's *Of the Sublime and the Beautiful.*

p. 187. *Grecian and Gothic architecture.* This passage enlarges on the parallel suggested by Gilpin on p. 184 above.

p. 188. *Salvator Rosa.* Italian painter, born near Naples in 1615, died in Rome, 1673. Most of his work presents nature in savage and sombre moods. See Introduction, p. 29.

Guido. Guido Reni (1575–1642), Italian painter, born in Bologna, and famous for the grace and elegance of his compositions.

Clump or belt. See Walpole: *On Modern Gardening*, p. 216 above.

NOTES ON SOME CRITICAL TERMS

(with special reference to their significance in the eighteenth century)

Augustan. The literature of the reign of Augustus Cæsar (27 B.C.–
A.D. 14), the period of Virgil, represented the high-water mark of
Latin literature. It was natural, therefore, that the term 'Augustan'
should be applied to the Queen Anne–George I period in England
and to its literature, for this period was strongly influenced by the
classical Latin models and presented a similar brilliant group of men
of letters. Perhaps the best-known application of the term was in
Goldsmith's essay on "The Augustan Age in England" in *The Bee*.
The use of the word to characterize this period became more
frequent in the nineteenth century.

Neo-Classic. This term was not used in the eighteenth century,
but is a convenient epithet to distinguish the modern classical
writers of the seventeenth century and Augustan age from the
Greek and Latin classical authors. In literary criticism the word is
useful to distinguish Renaissance and seventeenth-century critical
doctrine (often contemporarily attributed to Aristotle and Horace)
from the actual critical statements of classical authors.

The Rules. During the early years of the eighteenth century the
'rules' of drama and poetry were still often attributed to Aristotle.
But, apart from insisting on unity of action and dramatic propriety,
Aristotle laid down no *rules*. Horace gave more definite formulæ,
but the Rules were really the creation of Renaissance Italian and
French critics. Castelvetro first formulated the rule of the three
unities in 1570, and in the course of the following hundred years
Italian and French critics prescribed regulations for almost every
aspect of drama and poetry.

Imitation. The eighteenth century inherited this term from the
pseudo-Aristotelian tradition of the Renaissance. In its original
sense the word implied the copying or reproduction of natural forms
in art or letters. To this was added the meaning (as in Ascham, Ben
Jonson, or Reynolds) of close study of classical masters with a view

to producing similar excellence in English. In the early part of the eighteenth century the word usually meant more than mere copying, and implied what we should call "artistic representation"—the power to give new and imaginatively pleasurable form to ideas or images. The term gradually lost status in the century as greater stress came to be laid on invention, originality, and imagination.

Wit and Judgment: Fancy and Imagination. The term 'wit' had come to be used in the sixteenth century in the sense of the French *esprit*—range and originality of thought, intellectual quickness and subtlety. In the seventeenth century the meaning of the word tended to be narrowed to the power of finding clever (and often fanciful) images. The word thus denoted very much what Coleridge meant by 'fancy' (as distinguished from imagination), and was throughout the century opposed to 'judgment,' the rational faculty. Addison, in *The Spectator*, No. 62, quotes Locke's distinction between the two terms:

> For wit lying most in the assemblage of ideas, and putting those together with quickness and variety, wherein can be found any resemblance or congruity, thereby to make up pleasant pictures and agreeable visions in the fancy; judgment, on the contrary, lies quite on the other side, in separating carefully one from another, ideas wherein can be found the least difference, thereby to avoid being misled by similitude, and by affinity, to take one thing for another. This is a way of proceeding quite contrary to metaphor and allusion; wherein, for the most part, lies that entertainment and pleasantry of wit which strikes so lively on the fancy, and is therefore so acceptable to all people.

This passage from Locke's *Essay concerning the Human Understanding* (1690) throws light on the contemporary view of poetry. Neo-classical writers thought of poetic creation as a process in which the faculty of wit or fancy was joined with judgment or reason, the chief task of the author being to subject the liveliness of the fancy to the logic and order of judgment, and to maintain the predominance of the rational element in art over the imaginative.

The rise in importance and meaning of the term 'imagination' marked the superseding of this notion of art by more modern, and, as we think, sounder conceptions.

In the sixteenth and early seventeenth centuries 'imagination' denoted 'fantasy,' and often *morbid* fantasy. As the seventeenth century proceeded, the word came to be used indiscriminately with 'fancy' (though less frequently) to indicate the imaginative element in artistic creation; though the term 'invention' was normally used (as by Dryden) to indicate the basic creative element in art—the finding of the subject, the 'imitation of Nature' as distinct from the imitation of the classics.

Addison used 'fancy' and 'imagination' as synonymous, but from the *Spectator* essays onwards the latter term tended to predominate, and gradually acquired more of the modern meaning.

Lord Kames (1761) defined 'imagination' as the "singular power of fabricating images without any foundation in reality," and pointed out that the materials employed in this operation were ideas of sight; ideas derived from the other senses being much too obscure to be broken down and combined into new forms in this way. (*Cf.* Addison: *Spectator*, No. 411; p. 96 above.)

The word 'fancy,' on the other hand, depreciated until Coleridge (see *Biographia Literaria*, chapter xiii) fixed a permanent distinction between the two terms.

Taste. The use of this word in England, towards 1700, to denote cultivated artistic sensibility was doubtless influenced by the parallel use of the Italian *gusto* and French *goût*. It was first applied to the elegant amateur. In the early years of the century the term was frequently opposed to judgment—the man of taste who judged works of art by their appeal to his sensibility being regarded as superior to the mere critic who judged according to the Rules. (*Cf.* p. 168 above.) But gradually the notion of taste came to include power of judgment as well as sensibility. (*Cf.* note on p. 208.)

The significance of the word has never been exactly defined in modern English. Sir Joshua Reynolds, for example, indicates a different sense when he says that you might refer to Pope or Prior as poets marked by taste, but that the term would be inappropriate if applied to a sublime poet such as Homer or Milton.

Genius. In the seventeenth century 'genius' meant talent in a particular direction, a sense fairly close to its Latin etymology. But the word had never lost its original connexion with 'genius' in the sense of 'guardian spirit,' and thus always carried with it a suggestion of 'inspiration' (as, for example, in Sidney's *Apologie for Poetrie*). The neo-classical critics tried to 'play down' this element in the meaning of the word (*cf.* Johnson, *Rambler*, No. 154, and Reynolds, *Discourse VI*), but even they were forced to admit an inspired quality in the genius of Shakespeare. In the latter part of the century, and especially after Young's essay *On Original Composition*, there was an increasing tendency to magnify the idea of 'genius,' and to contrast it with mere 'talent' (a distinction made even more frequently in Germany and France than in England) so that Coleridge felt bound to protest against this exaggeration of one side of genius, and wrote the famous passage in which he set out to show that "Shakespeare's judgment was equal to his genius."

Nevertheless, the currency of the word 'genius' helped to secure recognition (from about 1760) of the primary place of the creative or imaginative element in poetry or art. Duff wrote, in his *Essay on Original Genius* (1767), ". . . creative Imagination is the distinguishing characteristic of true Genius."

Nature. In the earlier eighteenth century, and in the writings of Dr Johnson or Reynolds, the word embraced not only the physical world but also human life in all its aspects, social, intellectual, and spiritual. It was in this sense that Johnson spoke of Shakespeare as "holding the mirror up to nature." For the neo-classical critics, whose view of the universe was largely determined by the philosophy of Descartes and Locke, the word also denoted the order and structure characterizing the physical world, and the system or reason which lay behind it.

The Romantic poets and critics, on the other hand, tended to limit the term 'nature' to the physical world, and to attribute to this world qualities derived from Romantic literature. Thus nature began to be seen as coloured by human emotion or as possessing spiritual qualities of its own. Simultaneously with this literary view of nature there grew up the idea of nature as 'picturesque'—nature being regarded through the eyes of the painter or in comparison with his work.

Romantic. The term dates from 1659. Its main use in the seventeenth century was to describe what was unreal or far-fetched, what was akin to the incidents and characters of the French romances of the time. But the word was occasionally used, as by Pepys, of scenery or architecture, with a suggestion of the colourful and stirring imaginative world of the medieval romances. The eighteenth century took hold of this sense of the term, which became useful to describe literature or art which made its primary appeal to the imagination or to the senses and emotions; and since classical literature, on the other hand, was regarded as characterized by logical clarity, order, and reason, the terms 'Classic' and 'Romantic' naturally began to be looked upon as opposites. The distinction between the Romantic and classical in spirit or substance was

P

naturally linked with the historical meanings of these terms, the word 'Romantic' in this connexion referring to the medieval Northern literature of chivalry. The opposition between classical and Romantic in literary practice and literary theory was never as sharp or as bitter in England as in France and Germany.

Rococo. This word is presumably derived from the French *rocaille*, and for the last hundred years has been applied to furniture and architectural ornament of the Louis XIV and Louis XV period, which is characterized by an excess of conventional scroll-work and shell-decoration. It is interesting to note that when the term was first used in English, in about 1836, it was a colloquialism, and meant 'old-fashioned.'

Sentimental. Although the noun 'sentiment' had been used in English from medieval times, first in the sense of 'opinion' and later of 'feeling,' the adjective dates from about 1730. In the eighteenth century the word, as applied to persons, meant 'characterized by refined and elevated feeling'; and when used of works of art or literary compositions meant 'conveying refined æsthetic emotion' or 'appealing to the emotions' (especially of love). The present-day meaning of the word, implying superficiality, or excess or morbidity of feeling, grew up in the nineteenth century.

SOME BOOKS FOR REFERENCE AND FOR FURTHER STUDY

The Social Background

TREVELYAN, G. M.: *English Social History* (London, 1944) (see chapters x-xiv).

TURBERVILLE, G. S. (editor): *Johnson's England*, 2 vols. (Oxford, 1933).

The Philosophic Background

STEPHEN, L.: *History of English Thought in the 18th Century*, 2 vols. (London, 1876).

English Literature and Society in the 18th Century (London, 1904).

WILLEY, B.: *The Eighteenth Century Background* (London, 1940).

The History of Literature

GOSSE, E.: *History of 18th Century Literature (1660–1780)* (London, 1889).

PHELPS, W. L.: *Beginning of the English Romantic Movement* (Boston, 1893).

VAUGHAN, C. E.: *The Romantic Revolt* (Edinburgh, 1900).

REYNOLDS, M.: *The Treatment of Nature in English Poetry between Pope and Wordsworth* (revised edition, Chicago, 1912).

BAILEY, J. C.: *Dr Johnson and his Circle* (London, 1913).

ELTON, O.: *Survey of English Literature (1730–1788)* 2 vols. (London, 1928).

Literary Criticism and Æsthetics

KNIGHT, W.: *Philosophy of the Beautiful* (London, 1891).

BOSANQUET, B.: *A History of Æsthetic* (London, 1892).

GAYLEY, C. M. and SCOTT, F. N.: *An Introduction to the Methods and Materials of Literary Criticism* (Boston, 1899).

KER, W. P. (editor): *Essays of John Dryden*, 2 vols. (Oxford, 1900).

SAINTSBURY, G.: *History of English Criticism* (Edinburgh, 1911). *Loci Critici* (Boston, 1903).

SMITH, D. N. (editor): *Shakespearean Criticism of the 18th Century* (Glasgow, 1903).

SPRINGARN, J. E. (editor): *Critical Essays of the 17th Century*, 3 vols. (Oxford, 1908–9).

DURHAM, W. H. (editor): *Critical Essays of the 18th Century (1700– 1725)* (Yale, 1915).

ROBERTSON, J. C.: *Studies in the Genesis of Romantic Theory in the 18th Century* (Cambridge, 1923).

ELTON, O.: *Reason and Enthusiasm in the 18th Century* in *English Association Essays and Studies*, Vol. x (Oxford, 1924).

CLARK, A. F. B.: *Boileau and the French Classical Critics in England (1660–1830)* (Paris, 1925).

MANWARING, E. W.: *Italian Landscape in 18th Century England* (Oxford, 1925).

SMITH, L. P.: *Four Words: Romantic, Originality, Creative, Genius* in *Words and Idioms* (London, 1925).

HUSSEY, C.: *The Picturesque* (London, 1927).

MONK, S. H.: *The Sublime: a Study of Critical Theories in 18th Century England* (New York, 1935).

JONES, R. F.: *Ancients and Moderns: a Study of the Background of the 'Battle of the Books'* (St Louis, 1936).

ALLEN, B. S.: *Tides in English Taste 1619–1800: A Background for the Study of Literature* (Cambridge, U.S.A., 1937).

HOOKER, E. N. (editor): *Works of John Dennis*, 2 vols. (Baltimore, 1939).

WELLEK, R.: *The Rise of English Literary History* (University of N. Carolina, 1941).

BATE, W. J.: *From Classic to Romantic. Premises of Taste in Eighteenth Century England* (Harvard, 1946).

LOVEJOY, A. O.: *Nature as Æsthetic Norm* reprinted in *Essays in the History of Ideas* (John Hopkins University Press, 1948).

CARRITT, E. F.: *Calendar of British Taste, 1600–1800* (London, 1949).

The Arts and Art-theory

DRYDEN, J.: Translation of Du Fresnoy's *De Arte Graphica—The Art of Painting* (London, 1695).

RICHARDSON, JONATHAN: *Essays on the Theory of Painting* (London, 1715).

CAMPBELL, COLIN and OTHERS: *Vitruvius Britannicus*, 3 vols. (London, 1717–25).

GIBBS, J.: *Book of Architecture* (London, 1728).

LANGLEY, BATTY: *Gothic Architecture improved by Rules and Proportions. In Many Grand Designs* (London, 1742).

EDWARD, W. P. and DARLEY: *A New Book of Chinese Designs Calculated to Improve the Present Taste* (London, 1754).

WARE, ISAAC: *Complete Body of Architecture* (London, 1756).

ADAM, R. and J.: *Works in Architecture*, 3 vols. (London, 1778–1822).

BLOMFIELD, R.: *History of Renaissance Architecture in England*, 2 vols. (London, 1897).

GOTCH, J. A.: *The English Home, from Charles I to George IV* (London, 1918).

MULLINER, I. H.: *Decorative Arts in England, 1660–1780* (London, 1919).

JOURDAIN, M.: *English Decoration and Furniture of the later Eighteenth Century* (London, 1922).

CLARK, K.: *The Gothic Revival* (London, 1928).

LLOYD, N.: *The English House* (London, 1931, revised 1949).

STEGMAN, JOHN: *The Rule of Taste: George I–George IV* (London, 1936).

SUMMERSON, JOHN: *Georgian London* (London, 1945).

SITWELL, S.: *British Architects and Craftsmen, 1600–1830* (London, 1946).

RICHARDSON, A. E.: *Georgian Architecture* (New York, 1950).

Garden-design

LANGLEY, BATTY: *New Principles of Gardening* (London, 1728).

WHATELEY, R.: *Observations on Modern Gardening* (London, 1770).

CHAMBERS, SIR W.: *Dissertation on Oriental Gardening* (London, 1772).

REPTON, H.: *Sketches and Hints on Landscape Gardening* (London, 1795).
CHASE, I. W. W.: *Horace Walpole, Gardenist* (Princeton, 1943).
CLARK, H. F.: *The English Landscape Garden* (London, 1948).
STROUD, D.: *Capability Brown* (London, 1950).

Travel and Topography

DEFOE, D.: *A Tour through the whole Island of Great Britain*, 3 vols. (London, 1724–26). (Later editions edited by S. Richardson and others.)
GILPIN, W.: *Observations on the River Wye, relative chiefly to Picturesque Beauty* (London, 1782).
Observations on the Mountains and Lakes of Cumberland and Westmorland (London, 1786).
Observations on several parts of Great Britain, particularly the Highlands of Scotland (London, 1786).
Remarks on Forest Scenery and other Woodland Views (London, 1791).
Observations on the Western Parts of England (London, 1798).

Important Texts from which no Extracts are included in this Book

HUGHES, J.: Preface to edition of Spenser (London, 1715).
POPE, A.: Preface to Homer's *Iliad* (London, 1715).
Moral Essays, Epistle IV, to the Earl of Burlington (London, 1731).
SPENCE, J.: *Crito, or a Dialogue on Beauty* (London, 1725).
HUME, D.: *Treatise of Human Nature* (London, 1739).
Essay *On the Standard of Taste* in *Essays Moral, Political and Literary*, Vol. I (London, 1742).
AKENSIDE, M.: *The Pleasures of the Imagination* (London, 1744).
WARTON, J.: *The Enthusiast; or the Lover of Nature* (London, 1744).
HOGARTH, W.: *Analysis of Beauty* (London, 1753).
WARTON, T.: *Observations on the Faerie Queene* (London, 1754).
History of English Poetry (London, 1774–78).
SHEBBEARE, J.: *Letters on the English Nation*, 2 vols. (London, 1755).
REYNOLDS, SIR J.: Three Letters to *The Idler* (London, 1757).
GERARD, A.: *On Taste* (Edinburgh, 1758).
SMITH, A.: *The Theory of Moral Sentiments* (London, 1759).

KAMES, LORD: *Elements of Criticism*, 3 vols. (Edinburgh, 1762).

PERCY, T.: Preface to and Essays in *Reliques of Ancient English Poetry*, 3 vols. (London, 1765).

DUFF, W.: *Essay on Original Genius* (London, 1767).

MASON, W.: *The English Garden, A Poem* (Book I, Dublin, 1772; Books II, III, IV, York, 1777–81).

GERARD, A.: *Essay on Genius* (Edinburgh, 1774).

REID, T.: *Essay VIII: Of Taste* in *Essays on the Intellectual Powers of Man* (Edinburgh, 1790).

KNIGHT, R. P.: *The Landscape—a didactic poem in Three books* (London, 1794).